MODERN WORLD NATIONS

# Egypt

Joseph J. Hobbs
University of Missouri, Columbia

Series Consulting Editor
Charles F. Gritzner
South Dakota State University

CHELSEA HOUSE
PUBLISHERS
A Haights Cross Communications Company
Philadelphia

*Frontispiece:* Flag of Egypt

*Cover:* This 'Ababda Bedoiun of the Eastern Desert continues to maintain the lifestyle of the desert nomad.

*Dedication:* For Cindy, with love

## CHELSEA HOUSE PUBLISHERS

EDITOR IN CHIEF Sally Cheney
DIRECTOR OF PRODUCTION Kim Shinners
CREATIVE MANAGER Takeshi Takahashi
MANUFACTURING MANAGER Diann Grasse

### Staff for EGYPT

EDITOR Lee Marcott
PRODUCTION ASSISTANT Jaimie Winkler
COVER AND SERIES DESIGNER Takeshi Takahashi
LAYOUT 21st Century Publishing and Communications, Inc.
PHOTOS All images courtesy of Joseph Hobbs

A Haights Cross Communications Company

http://www.chelseahouse.com

First Printing

1 3 5 7 9 8 6 4 2

Library of Congress Cataloging-in-Publication Data

Hobbs, Joseph J. (Joseph John), 1956-
    Egypt / Joseph J. Hobbs.
       v. cm. — (Modern world nations)
Includes bibliographical references and index. Contents: Introducing Egypt—Egypt's natural landscapes—Egypt through time—People and culture—Government—Economy—Living in Egypt today—Egypt looks ahead.
    ISBN 0-7910-6931-1 — ISBN 0-7910-7178-2 (pbk.)
    1. Egypt—Juvenile literature. [1. Egypt.] I. Title. II. Series.
DT49 .H63 2002
962—dc21
                                                                    2002007323

# Table of Contents

# Egypt

Modern downtown Cairo, on the banks of the Nile River, is home to the city's main government offices and tourist hotels. Close by are some of Cairo's more affluent neighborhoods.

# Introducing Egypt

O n September 11, 2001, two large passenger jets slammed into the World Trade Center towers in New York City, and a third plane struck the Pentagon in Washington, D.C. Within days, U.S. intelligence sources traced the attacks and another that caused the crash of a plane in rural Pennsylvania to al-Qaida, an organization financed by a Saudi Arabian named Osama bin Laden. But bin Laden's right-hand man, the one believed to responsible for planning the attack, was an Egyptian. Some of the hijackers of the planes were Egyptian. As American planes began bombing targets associated with Osama bin Laden in Afghanistan, some Egyptians took to the streets of Cairo in protest against the United States. Egypt seemed to be living up to its reputation as a hotbed of Islamic unrest and a breeding ground for terrorism.

That is the Egypt in the news now. But open up a *National*

*Geographic* magazine, a coffee-table book about the wonders of the world, or a book on Western civilization, and a different Egypt can be seen. It is a land of temples and tombs, of pharaohs and pyramids, of camels and sand. It is a photogenic and mysterious land, so unlike the United States, yet somehow linked to the American way of life—it is the birthplace of paper and written language, of monumental architecture, and of irrigation.

And there is an Egypt many in the United States have probably not seen, the homeland of the 70 million generous, gregarious, and proud people that today call themselves Egyptians. They are Muslim and Christian, city dweller, village peasant, and desert nomad. Some are wealthy, but most are not. Nearly all of them, though, have one custom in common: If they were to see a stranger passing by their home, they would cry out "*ahlan wa sahlan*"—"welcome!" and beckon that person to come meet them and enjoy their hospitality.

How can people understand these different Egypts? How can a culture of hospitality and generosity produce people that hate and destroy? How can so much have been accomplished so long ago in a country that is almost completely barren desert? And what does the West owe to that ancient culture? By answering these and other questions, this book will introduce the extraordinary country that is Egypt.

Look at Egypt—officially known as the Arab Republic of Egypt—on a world map. One obvious feature is the country's central location relative to the continents of Africa, Asia, and Europe. If the Middle East is the crossroads of the three continents, then Egypt is the crossroads of those crossroads. In the very distant past, the first humans came out of Africa to populate Asia and Europe. They would have passed through Egypt. Cultures, ideas, and materials have crisscrossed Egypt for thousands of years, leaving their mark on land and life in Egypt, and often borrowing Egyptian elements. By sea, the shortest distance between Europe and the Far East is through the Mediterranean Sea, the Suez Canal, and the Red Sea—through Egypt. Egypt's

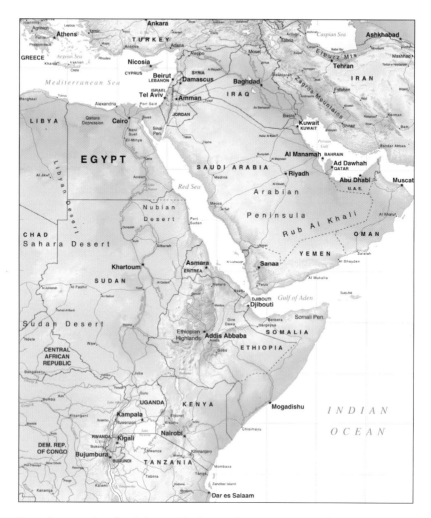

Egypt is an ancient land situated in the northeastern corner of Africa, between the Mediterranean and Red Seas. Modern Egypt has played a pivotal role in the Arab nations, in the larger world of the African continent, and in the world of Islam. It has also served to link Asia with the rest of Africa.

Suez Canal is one of the world's most important waterways, and keeping it open to international sea traffic is essential to the economic well being of many countries.

Look closely at the map again. Notice that Egypt occupies portions of two continents. In the extreme northeast is the triangular peninsula called Sinai, which sits in Asia. The Suez

Canal marks the dividing line between Asia and Africa. Leaving Sinai—Asia, that is—one can actually drive through a tunnel beneath the canal and emerge a few seconds later in Africa. That is where most of Egypt is.

Driving westward from the Suez Canal one would cross mostly flat, open desert country for about two hours. This is the Eastern Desert. There are no villages or towns, only a few bus stops and coffee shops. Then the landscape begins to change. Factories first, then some apartment blocks . . . more and more traffic . . . above, a brownish haze. Soon there are high-rise buildings standing side by side, and traffic comes to a crawl. This is Cairo. With almost 20 million people it is the largest city in Africa and in the Middle East. This area is also the Nile Valley. The drive from the eastern outskirts of Cairo to its downtown on the banks of the Nile takes less than an hour. Cairo is the heart of Egypt—the great city Egyptians call *Umm ad-Dunya*, the "the Mother of the World."

The Greek historian Herodotus called Egypt "the gift of the Nile." The river has always been Egypt's lifeblood, and certainly if not for it Egypt would probably be no more world-famous than, say, Chad or Chile. Egypt without the Nile would also be a country with few people. The Nile has deposited some of the world's best agricultural soils along its floodplain, and for thousands of years Egypt has been a prolific producer of cereal crops, fruits, and vegetables. Until quite recently, Egypt was able to produce more than enough food for the people living on the shores of the Nile. And even today, that is where 9 out of every 10 Egyptians live. A map showing the population distribution in Egypt is astonishing—the dots representing thousands of people create a perfect outline map of the Nile River and the Nile Delta on the Mediterranean, and there are few dots elsewhere.

Driving north from Cairo, there are the lush cotton fields and numerous cities and villages of the delta. It is possible to reach the Mediterranean Sea in about four hours. The roads south along the Nile pass through bright green fields and

This aerial view shows the Nile Valley, where most Egyptians live. The Nile River snakes through the floodplain.

innumerable settlements, mostly villages—southern Egypt is more rural and poorer than the north. After a three-day trip, the Nile Valley stops at the frontier city of Aswan. It has a distinctively African feeling, and while the weather in the previous places you visited was warm, it is now hot. The Nubian people that live here are darker skinned than the Egyptians downstream (to the north), and many goods in Aswan's markets are from sub-Saharan Africa. South of town there is a giant dam blocking the Nile River, and stretching southward from it all the way into the Sudan is a great reservoir, Lake Nasser.

West of the Nile Valley along its entire course through

The Great Sand Sea of the Western Desert is a vast expanse of lifeless wilderness that covers hundreds of square miles.

Egypt is another desert, even more arid and forbidding than the one between the Suez Canal and Cairo. It is the Western Desert. There are a few oases, green islands of date palms rising from a desert sea, where people do live, but except for these and a thin line of settlements along the Mediterranean coast, the Western Desert is a vast uninhabited wilderness stretching from the Nile to Libya.

Egypt is thus a geographically "simple" country: a densely populated river valley cuts through almost unpopulated deserts. In political and cultural terms, Egypt is richer and more complex. To appreciate its place in the world, it is necessary to begin by recognizing that its population is quite large for a country its size (deserts included). Egypt's 70 million people make up almost a quarter of the population of the Middle East. Just in demographic terms, then, Egypt carries a lot of importance in the region and offers a good pulse of the body that is the Middle East. Egypt is the cultural capital of the Middle East. In the Middle East, Cairo is like Hollywood and Nashville combined, producing films and music that audiences across the Arabic-speaking world devour. A mostly Muslim country, Egypt is also a fount of Islamic scholarship and civilization. When leading Egyptian clerics speak on important issues, their words travel as far west as Morocco and east to Indonesia.

Egypt's voice in international political affairs is also strong. Egypt was the first Arab country to make peace with Israel, the long-time adversary of the Arab world. It was a risky move. In signing a peace treaty, Egypt earned the status it retains today as a reasonable, moderate, reliable country; a friend of the West in a region where many countries are known for radicalism, strife, and anti-Western sentiment. But the peace treaty also angered many within Egypt and throughout the Middle East who believed that Arabs should never make peace with the Israeli enemy. As the United States rewarded Egypt for its peacemaking with large amounts of economic aid, and gradually placed more and more soldiers and military assets in the region, much of the growing anger was also directed against the United States. And then came September 11.

It is time to explore Egypt, this land of war and peace, river and desert, Islam and Christianity, antiquity and modernity. Travel through its natural landscapes, survey its rich history, and see how Egyptians live and how they view the world. Find out why the country is struggling economically and wrestling with political problems. Finally, look to the future of this "antique land," as the British poet Shelley called Egypt.

A man cranks the shaft of an Archimedean screw, which draws water up the metal column from the canal to the irrigated field.

CHAPTER

2

# Natural Landscapes

M ost of Egypt is situated in the northeast corner of Africa, but Egypt also includes southwest Asia's Sinai Peninsula. The country extends about 1,170 miles (1,970 kilometers) south to north from about 22 to 32 degrees north latitude—so, only south-ernmost Egypt is in the tropics—and 760 miles (1,260 kilometers) west to east from about 25 to 35 degrees east longitude. Egypt's total area is 386,662 square miles (1,001,450 square kilometers), or about the area of Texas, Oklahoma, and New Mexico. Egypt's neighbors are Libya to the west, Israel to the northeast, and Sudan to the south. The Mediterranean Sea's shoreline is the northern border, while the Gulf of Suez and Red Sea make up the eastern border of mainland Egypt. The Sinai Peninsula forms a narrow wedge between Africa and Asia and is framed by the Mediterranean Sea on the north, the Isthmus of Suez and Gulf of Suez on the west, and the Gulf of Aqaba and Israeli border on the east.

Egypt has a hot desert climate. As the country is in the lower middle latitudes of the Northern Hemisphere, the highest temperatures are in the summer months of June through August, and the coldest period is December through February. From north to south across Egypt, there are three climatic zones. The Mediterranean coast belt gets between three and eight inches (70 to 200 millimeters) of rain each year and has a January average low temperature of 48°F (9°C) and an average July maximum temperature of 86°F (30°C). The Middle Egypt belt (southward to about 29 degrees north latitude) gets only up to about one and a half inches (35 millimeters) of rain yearly (in Cairo) and has only slightly higher temperatures than the Mediterranean zone. The Upper Egypt belt, where rainfall is scarce indeed, typically gets between no rainfall to one-tenth of an inch (three millimeters) per year. People living anywhere in the eastern two-thirds of the United States get far more rain from a single thunderstorm than southern (Upper) Egypt will get in 10 years. It is hot there, too: At the southern Nile city of Aswan, the average low temperature in January is 49°F (9.3°C), and the average July high is a torrid 108°F (42°C). During the season the Egyptians call *khamsiin* (meaning 50 days) during March through May, hot Saharan winds cause sandstorms across the country, making even northern cities like Cairo feel Aswan-like for a few days.

These are the broad features of Egypt's climate, but local conditions vary a lot where there are mountains, especially in the Sinai Peninsula and in easternmost mainland Egypt. Temperatures fall with higher elevations and can be determined by using this formula for mountains anywhere: by about 3.6°F (2°C) per 1,000 feet (305 meters). The mountains tend to "make" rain, too—an effect geographers call orographic precipitation— so Egypt's highlands are wetter and have more vegetation than lower regions. Still, these are desert mountains and Egypt is a desert country.

Egypt's main natural landscape regions are the Nile Valley, the Nile Delta, and the Suez Canal Zone; the North Coast, the Western Desert, and the Eastern Desert; and the Sinai Peninsula. The following journey will illustrate how people who have occupied Egypt for a very long time have used and changed these landscapes.

### The Nile Valley, the Nile Delta, and the Suez Canal Zone

Within the desert that is Egypt, the Nile Valley is a long, thin oasis. While the deserts, which the ancients called the Red Land, make up about 96 percent of the country, human life in Egypt has always been focused on the fertile Black Land along the river. Despite its vast wilderness, Egypt is synonymous with civilization; its Arabic name, *Masr*, comes from the verb meaning "to found, build, settle, civilize, colonize." And that civilization is synonymous with the Nile.

The Nile River has two sources, one in highland Ethiopia at Lake Tana, which feeds the Blue Nile, and the other in Central Africa around Lake Victoria, which feeds the White Nile. At their junction at Khartoum, Sudan, the Blue Nile accounts for about 70 percent of the river's summer high-season volume. Until contained by two 20th-century dams at Aswan, the surge of summer rainwater from the fertile Ethiopian highlands inundated much of Egypt's Nile floodplain every August and September. Each flood left a deposit of about 1/20 of an inch (1 millimeter) of silt yearly, building very fertile sediments that are now about 25 feet (8 meters) deep.

Nearly all of Egypt's farmland is found in that 14,000 square mile (35,000 square kilometer) "river oasis" consisting of the Nile Valley, known traditionally as Upper Egypt, and the Nile Delta, known as Lower Egypt. The Nile runs almost due north, so in Egypt it is necessary to switch the usual orientation and think of south as up. The green ribbon of the Nile Valley is narrow, only about 6 miles (10 kilometers) wide on average. Escarpments, or cliffs, of sandstone and limestone up to 1,000 feet high (305 meters) trace long stretches of the valley's desert borders. There is a break in this cliff wall southwest of Cairo, where a canal carries Nile water into a fertile depression called the Faiyum.

The transformation of the Egyptian Nile from a natural to a cultural landscape has been in progress for over 7,000 years. Around 5000 B.C.E., Neolithic people in the Faiyum saw perhaps half the river's floodplain covered with savanna grasses and dry thickets. In these habitats the people grazed domestic sheep, goats, pigs, and cattle, and hunted elephant and hartebeest (African antelope). From the river, they took Nile perch and other fish, trapped birds, and hunted hippopotamus and crocodile. They grew barley and emmer wheat, planting their crops after the annual floodwaters retreated in late October. They left the land fallow after the May harvest—the Nile was far down in its channel, and it was difficult to lift up enough water to plant a second summer crop.

With some improvements, this simple technology of seasonal flood irrigation sustained the civilization of Pharaonic Egypt (3100-332 B.C.E.). The conversion to permanent, or perennial, irrigation began modestly around 1500 B.C.E. with the introduction of the *shaduf,* a device for lifting water to summer crops. It brought increasing amounts of floodplain wildlands into cultivation. The pace of change quickened under Greek and Roman rule (332 B.C.E. to 324 A.D.). Unused regions of Upper Egypt and the Faiyum were settled and planted with wheat, barley, broad beans, millet, sesame, lentils, clover, and flax. Other water lifting devices, like the Archimedean screw and water wheel, were used to irrigate more land along the Nile and its canals. The limit of cultivation set by the technology available was almost reached, with the planted area almost equal to what was planted 2,000 years later, in 1880. Agricultural improvements were accompanied by population growth, with the number of Egyptians doubling in 300 years to almost five million in 50 A.D.

The large-scale change from basin to perennial irrigation began in modern times after 1800, with the building of barrages, low barriers across the Nile that lifted water for movement through canals to irrigate summer crops downstream. Then, in

Cattle have been among Egypt's main livestock animals for thousands of years.

1902, a dam was built to actually store water for use in the summer. This was the low dam placed at Aswan, in southern Egypt. The final conversion to perennial irrigation came with the construction of the Aswan High Dam, completed in 1970.

Upstream from the Aswan High Dam, a reservoir called Lake Nasser stretches 295 miles (490 kilometers) south to the Sudan. As it formed, this lake drowned a region known historically as Nubia. Except for some of the larger and more famous buildings that were relocated to higher ground, many ancient Egyptian monuments were lost beneath the rising waters. Nubians, the people who lived along the river, had to be relocated to new settlements. Some of them have since returned to the shores of Lake Nasser to fish and farm, and they often compete with crocodiles.

The Nile Delta fans out below Cairo, where the river divides into two branches or distributaries, the Rosetta and Damietta, named for the two towns situated at their respective mouths. The delta forms a rough triangle with a height of 100 miles

The Aswan Low Dam was built in 1902 to hold water for summer crop irrigation. The dam is situated where granite rocks force the Nile River into narrow rapids.

(170 kilometers) from its 130-mile (220-kilometer) long base on the Mediterranean to its apex near Cairo. Its area is 8,800 square miles (22,000 square kilometers) (compared with the Nile Valley's 5,200 square miles, or 13,000 square kilometers), or 63 percent of Egypt's inhabited terrain. Along the delta coast is a chain of elongated lakes, from west to east: Maryut, Idku, Burullus, and Manzala. These are brackish (slightly salty) and shallow bodies of water, generally less than three feet (one meter) deep, joined directly to the sea by narrow channels through sandbars and limestone ridges.

As many as seven Nile distributaries once snaked across the delta to create a network of river arms, islands, seasonally flooded basins, and swamps. Around 5000 B.C.E., Neolithic people exploited the Nile Delta much as they did the Nile Valley, planting crops, herding animals, and fishing and fowling in the wetlands. During early Pharaonic times (about 2700-2300 B.C.E.),

Fishermen leave their boats on the shore of Lake Manzala, one of several bodies of water along the Nile Delta.

ancient Egyptians called the wetlands the "bird tanks of pleasure" and the "papyrus lands." Wealthy men hunted birds for sport in these areas, where papyrus and lotus were the most commonly found plants.

People eventually tamed the delta wildlands, although later than they did the Nile Valley. Beginning around 300 B.C.E, Greek and later Roman colonists developed the region, turning marshes into vineyards and orchards, and establishing new towns. Pressure on the wetlands intensified. Eventually even papyrus, the Pharaonic symbol of Lower Egypt, became extinct there. The demand for paper products had resulted in its widescale cultivation, and it also grew wild. But the plant was doomed once linen paper was substituted for papyrus in the 10th century. Papyrus was uprooted to make way for new agricultural land. It was gone by 1821.

Nearly adjoining the eastern delta is the Suez Canal Zone. An almost continuous strip of green land borders the 90-mile (150-kilometer) canal between the cities of Port Said on the

Mediterranean Sea and Suez on the Gulf of Suez. The canal itself is made up of artificial excavations in sandy plains and of the natural bodies of Lake Timsah and the Great and Little Bitter Lakes. Another important city in the canal zone is Ismailiya, known as Egypt's garden city.

Ever since the Canal was completed there has been an open exchange of marine life between the Red Sea and the Mediterranean. Before the canal was completed in 1869, animals migrated back and forth across the Isthmus of Suez. By this means, for example, the flightless ostrich reached Asia from Africa. Most large mammals found east of the Nile in Egypt are also found in southwest Asia. The canal today is probably making such wildlife exchanges more difficult.

Because of the intense human activity on the landscape, the wildlife of the Nile Valley, the Nile Delta, and the Suez Canal Zone today is very poor. Migratory birds are trapped in vast numbers during the autumn for sale as food items. The main mammals are those that farmers have accepted as neighbors and those best at avoiding contact with people: hedgehog, shrew, jackal, fox, mongoose, jungle cat, and wild cat. Domesticated animals have taken the place of the large wild animals. Rural people of the Nile Valley and delta share their land with cattle, water buffalo, camels, donkeys, sheep, and goats. The pesticides they use to farm have eliminated some birds of prey and other predators, allowing rats to grow in number. There are very few wild plants and trees. Trees grow mainly on the margins of fields, canals, and roads and include the native date palm and tamarisk, and the introduced Australian pine.

## Desert Regions

Egypt's deserts—the Western Desert, the Eastern Desert, and the Sinai—make up most of the country's area and were not always as dry as they are today. The Neolithic period from 8000-3000 B.C.E. was generally a time of more rains. As much as 4 to 12 inches (100 to 300 millimeters) fell each year west of the

This pelican, trapped during its fall migration, is on sale at a Port Said market. These birds are brought to market to be sold as food.

Nile, creating semiarid shrub habitats similar to those found in tropical northeast Africa today. During that time, people probably kept cattle and grew crops on what is now completely barren land. They also hunted game animals, including the giraffe. East of the Nile, where there were abundant winter rains, hunters pursued elephants and other savanna game animals. But the rainy period ended about 2400 B.C.E., and Egypt's climate has been extremely dry ever since. The savanna grasses gave way to desert scrub and barren land. Animals with high water requirements became locally extinct. Some people retreated to places of permanent water in the Western Desert oases and along the Nile. Others adjusted to the changing conditions by practicing a pastoral nomadic livelihood (described in chapter 4), in which they moved with their livestock in search of water and vegetation.

### The Western Desert

The Western Desert, sometimes called the Libyan Desert, encompasses 272,400 square miles (681,000 square kilometers), or about two-thirds of Egypt's total area. East to west, it extends from the Nile Valley to the Libyan border, and south to north from the Sudanese border to the Mediterranean Sea. It consists of several plateaus of limestone and sandstone, a vast area of sand, and several depressions that contain oases.

The Western Desert does not have spectacular mountains such as are in the Sinai Peninsula and Eastern Desert. The highest point is 6,244 feet (1,892 meters) on Jebel Uweinat, a sandstone and igneous range spanning the extreme southwestern corner of Egypt. This is an unusual region in the sterile Western Desert. Rain falls once every 7 to 10 years, feeding small springs and supporting plants and animals similar to those found on the other side of the Nile, in the mountainous Eastern Desert. North of Jebel Uweinat is the Gilf Kebir, a divided sandstone plateau rising to 3,300 feet (1,000 meters). The Western Desert's largest natural region is a limestone plateau about 1,650 feet (500 meters) high, rising north of Gilf Kebir and stretching all the way from the Libyan border to the Nile Valley. It is rather lifeless except when rain falls at intervals of only once every 10 years or more, producing patches of "accidental" plant cover.

The Great Sand Sea is a vast body of sand stretching about 480 miles (800 kilometers) north to south from Siwa Oasis to Gilf Kebir, and 120 miles (200 kilometers) west to east from the Libyan border to Farafra Oasis. It consists mainly of almost lifeless sand dunes.

People rarely set foot on this desert wilderness, and it has long been a barrier to trade and movement. The Greek historian Herodotus claimed that 50,000 Persian soldiers died

The Bahariya Oasis is typical of the Western Desert oasis depressions. Bubbling springs support date palms and other crops. The limestone ridge that is the depression's rim can be seen in the distance.

trying to cross it when a ferocious sandstorm overtook them.

Embedded in the Western Desert's limestone plateau are several great oases depressions, the main locations of life in the Western Desert. Their formation began during ancient periods of abundant rainfall, when water widened fractures in the plateau floor. Winds then carved some of these fissures deeper and deeper, finally cutting into water-bearing levels in the limestone rock. This process created the principal oases and depressions of the Western Desert: Wadi el Natrun, Siwa Oasis, Qattara Depression, Bahariya Oasis, Farafra Oasis, and Dakhla Oasis. The typical Western Desert depression is nearly or completely encircled by steep cliffs, or escarpments. Its floor is near or below sea level. There are some good soils, and where water breaks the surface as springs there is a productive irrigated agriculture. In poorly drained low-lying areas of the depression floors, excess water accumulates in salty lakes surrounded by salt marshes, and farming is impossible. Aside from the oases depressions, the only agriculturally productive area of the Western Desert is its narrow coastal zone along the Mediterranean Sea. There, in a strip about 20 miles (32 kilometers) wide paralleling the sea from the Libyan border to Alexandria, relatively good rains support many crops and about half of all the wild plant species recorded in Egypt. Wild animals are scarce. The larger ones, such as the cheetah, oryx antelope, addax antelope. and hartebeest, were hunted to local extinction in the 20th century.

### The Eastern Desert

Also known as the Arabian Desert, the Eastern Desert is bounded by the Nile Valley to the west, the Nile Delta and Suez Isthmus to the north, the Gulf of Suez and Red Sea to the east, and the Sudan border to the south. The total area is 82,900 square miles (223,000 square kilometers), equal to 21 percent of Egypt's total area and one-third the area of the Western Desert. The region is made up of the Red Sea coastal plain, a north-south range of mountains, and several limestone and sandstone plateaus. The rugged mountain range contains the highest peak in Egypt outside Sinai, Jebel Shayib al-Banat (7,217 feet, or 2,187 meters). The Eastern Desert is very dry in general, with a vegetation of desert grasses, woody trees, and scrub limited to the valley floors. But the high mountains intercept cloud moisture, producing a rather more productive set of plant communities in the high elevations and in the larger drainages separating the mountain ranges. Characteristic mammals of these mountains and the plateaus to the west are the sand fox, hyena, sand cat, hyrax (looks like a large rodent, but is related to the elephant), ibex (shrew), Barbary sheep, and dorcas gazelle. Jebel Elba, a mountain in the extreme south near the Sudanese border, gets more rain than anywhere else in the Eastern Desert and has abundant plant and animal life, including ostrich and leopards that sometimes follow rains across the border from the Sudan. Overall then, while it is a desert wilderness, the Eastern Desert has more water and wildlife resources than the Western Desert (except for the oases), and pastoral nomads (see chapter 4) are able to make a living there.

### *The Sinai Peninsula*

The Sinai Peninsula is a triangle of 24,400 square miles (61,000 square kilometers) with its base along the Mediterranean Sea and its vertex, Ras Muhammad, jutting into the Red Sea. It is bordered on the west by the Suez Canal and the Gulf of Suez, and on the east by the Gulf of Aqaba and Egypt's 120-mile (200-kilometer) long political border with Israel. Sinai's Mediterranean coast has shallow lagoons, sand dunes, sandy plains, and salt marshes. The rest of the peninsula is physically an extension of the Eastern Desert, with coastal plains along the Gulfs of Suez and Aqaba, a core of high igneous mountains, plateaus of limestone and sandstone, and aprons of gravel plains draining and flanking the highlands. Just off the Gulf of Aqaba shore and at Ras Muhammad are coral reefs that are world famous among divers and snorkelers. Most of these are protected with national parks.

The mountainous interior of south Sinai contains Egypt's highest mountain, Jebel Katarina (8,715 feet, or 2,641 meters). Another prominent peak is Jebel Musa (7,524 feet, or 2,280 meters), widely believed to be the Mount Sinai of the Bible. Sinai's alpine topography accounts for relatively high precipitation—including rainfall—and a variety of plant and animal life. These mountains sustain about half of Sinai's roughly 1,000 plant species, which, in turn, make up 40 percent of the total flora of Egypt. Many are endemic, meaning they are found nowhere else in the world. Mammals include foxes, gazelles, and hyenas, but leopards were hunted to local extinction in the 1900s. With its more abundant water and vegetation, Sinai has an even larger population of pastoral nomads than does the Eastern Desert. Chapter 4 introduces them and Egypt's other diverse peoples.

The Great Sphinx, with the Pyramid of Cephren in the background, stands with Egypt's pyramids in Giza outside of Cairo.

# CHAPTER

# 3

# Journey
# Through Time

Egypt had one of the world's earliest civilizations, a way of life centered on cities. Archaeologists are still in the process of learning exactly how and why Egyptians made the transition from being nomadic hunters and gatherers to simple farmers and then diverse inhabitants of cities. It is certain that the productivity of early agriculture along the Nile played an important role in this transformation. Increasing output of food crops allowed more people to be fed. Then a growing population was able to find new ways to make agriculture more productive. Social scientists believe that there was also a relationship between agriculture and politics in ancient Egypt. A stratified, ranked society developed under the leadership of strong regional authorities. These leaders determined how and where irrigation canals should be dug, what crops should be planted, and how harvested crops should be distributed.

At the dawn of recorded history in Egypt, around 3200 B.C.E., there were really two Egypts under the control of men who made these kinds of decisions: Lower Egypt (the Nile Delta), with a king seated at the chief city of Buto, and Upper Egypt (the Nile Valley) with its king at Nekhen. Egyptian historians have found that the two kingdoms were united for the first time about 3100 B.C.E. by a warrior king named Menes (or Narmer). For almost the next 3,000 years the Egyptian king, called pharaoh, was depicted wearing the "double crown" of Upper and Lower Egypt. There are many other symbols of Egypt's unity, including the papyrus plant of Lower Egypt and the lotus plant of Upper Egypt, and the cobra of Lower Egypt and the vulture of Upper Egypt.

The king of Egypt was at the peak of a society and an economic system that were very creative and productive. From very early times, Egyptians made extraordinary achievements in art, architecture, literature, astronomy, medicine, mathematics, engineering, shipbuilding, and metallurgy. Many of these accomplishments actually peaked in the earliest stage of historical ancient Egypt: the pyramids, for example, were built in the Old Kingdom, around 2600 B.C.E.

In about 280 B.C.E. an Egyptian historian named Manetho came up with the ancient Egyptian chronology that is still used today. He divided the historical periods into the Old Kingdom (which modern historians date from 2700 to 2200 B.C.E.), the Middle Kingdom (2050-1800 B.C.E.) and the New Kingdom (1570-1090 B.C.E.). Between the Old and Middle Kingdom came the First Intermediate period, and between the Middle Kingdom and New Kingdom came the Second Intermediate period. Manetho identified 30 royal family lines, or dynasties, that ruled during these times; the New Kingdom, for example, was the time of the 18th, 19th, and 20th Dynasties.

During the Old Kingdom (the Third through Sixth Dynasties), the pharaoh ruled the two lands from Memphis, a city near modern Cairo. He enjoyed more power in this period

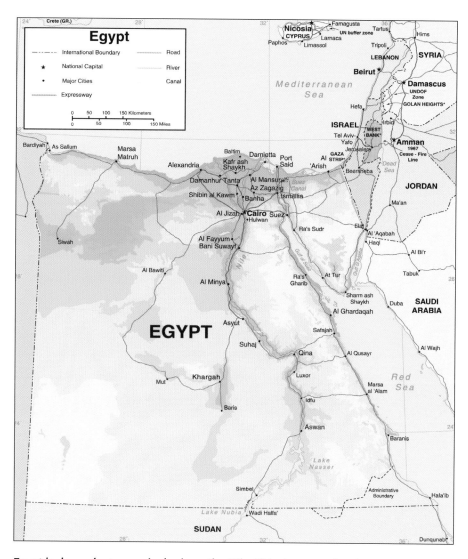

Egypt is dependent on a single river—the Nile. This river supplies the water that enables the civilization of Egypt to exist and also creates the floodplain where nearly all crops are cultivated and where 95 percent of the people live.

than in any other time of Egyptian history. Not only was he their supreme leader, but Egyptians also considered him a living god. Ancient Egyptian religion was very complex and included numerous gods, but the highest ranking ones included the sun-god Ra and the pharaoh, and these two were often merged

This ancient drawing shows the jackal-headed deity Anubis making an offering to Pharaoh Seti I, who wears the "double crown" of Upper and Lower Egypt.

into a single supreme deity. During the peaceful, prosperous days of the Old Kingdom, Egypt's peasant farmers worked the land from the end of the flood in October until the April harvest. A great many of them spent the other half of the year working in giant public works projects, including not only canals, but also monuments such as the pyramids. Contrary to many widely held theories, the fundamental purpose of the pyramid was to serve as the pharaoh's tomb. Nearby were the much smaller tombs, called *mastabas*, of the lesser royal family members and the wealthy noblemen that served the king. One of Egypt's richest archaeological sites is the Memphis cemetery of Saqqara, not far from the major pyramids at Giza, where the nobles of the Sixth Dynasty were buried. From decorations inside their mastabas, we can learn much about the daily life and the natural history of ancient Egypt. We see men fishing and catching birds in the marshes, and others hunting antelopes in the desert. They also show women dancing, children playing with pets, people mourning at funerals, craftsmen making jewelry and pottery, and farmers harvesting barley.

The tranquility of the Old Kingdom was followed by civil conflict, droughts, and perhaps even famine during the First Intermediate period. But order was restored during the Middle Kingdom, when many of Egypt's accomplishments were focused on Middle Egypt, or the central part of the Nile Valley between modern Minya and Asyut. Disorder followed in the Second Intermediate period as Egypt was invaded by the Hyksos, people from what is now Syria. The first pharaoh of the New Kingdom expelled these foreigners and prosperity returned to Egypt. Its rulers eventually were able to build an empire that extended as far east as Iraq. Foreign lands ruled by Egypt had to pay the Egyptians tribute, which is a kind of tax in the form of foods, minerals, and other commodities. Much of the wealth was funneled into the hands of a class of priests who, along with the pharaoh, effectively controlled the empire from the Upper Egyptian city of Thebes (modern Luxor).

Egypt's most colorful and controversial king was named Amenhotep IV (1369-1353 B.C.E.). Like his predecessors he began his rule from Thebes. But he resented the power of the priests, and he rejected the supremacy of their chief god, a regional deity named Amon. Amenhotep IV, who took his name from that god, then made a complete break with Amon and the Theban priests. He insisted there was only one god, the sun-god Aten. He renamed himself Akhenaten after that god and moved Egypt's capital to an obscure place in Middle Egypt. Akhenaten fostered a new, more informal style of art and apparently of human relationships, too. In contrast with the stiff, formal, and heroic portrayal of most kings, he had himself depicted as a rather paunchy, unattractive man, but a caring person who loved his wife (the famous Nefertiti) and children dearly.

Such tender scenes of royal family life may also be seen in the artifacts recovered from the tomb of Egypt's most famous king, Tutankhamen, who was probably the son of Akhenaten. "Tut" was a minor figure who assumed the throne as a boy after Akhenaten's death. The real power behind the throne was with the priests and the military, who returned Egypt's capital to Thebes. Tutankhamen died there and was buried in a tiny tomb that was soon forgotten. It was his obscurity that secured Tutankhamen's ultimate fame, for all of the other, much larger royal tombs in the Valley of Kings were robbed in ancient times, while Tut's remained sealed for more than 3,000 years. Only in 1922 did the English archaeologist Howard Carter breach the tomb's entrance and thrust in a candle to behold what he called "wonderful things."

Another of the New Kingdom's most famous pharaohs was Ramses II (Ramses the Great), who built colossal monuments to himself throughout the land (including Abu Simbel in Nubia) and waged wars against Egypt's Asian enemies. Egypt reached its peak of power in the "Ramesside" times of Ramses II and his immediate successors. Then the sun began to set on the glories of ancient Egypt. During what is known as the Late Dynastic period (1090 to 332 B.C.E.) invaders came from Libya, Sudan, Ethiopia, Assyria (modern Iraq), and Persia (modern Iran). The brilliant, young Macedonian Greek king Alexander the Great conquered Egypt in 332 B.C.E., beginning the era of Greek control known as the Ptolemaic period. The Ptolemaic rulers saw themselves as sympathetic benefactors of the Egyptian people and even merged many Egyptian gods and beliefs with their own. They built the great city of Alexandria, which for a time was the world's leading center of learning and the arts. A great library stood there until it burned down in the first century A.D. The last Ptolemaic ruler was the famous queen Cleopatra (Cleopatra VI). Through her strong will and

Egyptian was one of the world's first written languages, using mainly
pictures, or hieroglyphs, to tell a story. These hieroglyphs adorn a
temple in Luxor.

In the burial chamber of King Tutankhamen (ca. 1350 B.C.E.), a priest wearing a leopard skin is performing the "opening of the mouth" ceremony on the pharaoh's mummy.

personal relationships she was able for three decades to hold off the Romans from their most fervent desire: to conquer and control Egypt. Cleopatra was the last monarch to wear the double crown, and in that sense 3,000 years of ancient Egyptian history ended with her suicide in 30 B.C.E.

With Cleopatra's death, Egypt became a province of Rome and was ruled from that center of power. In contrast with the Greek Ptolemaic effort to build strong and friendly ties with the Egyptians, the Romans truly subjugated them. Rome saw Egypt as a colony from which it could take what it needed. Above all, Egypt was to serve as the granary of Rome, providing the motherland with cereal crops and other agricultural produce. Roman agents collected the exotic wildlife of Egypt and lands further south for the arena games held in Rome. Gold and valuable types of building and ornamental stone were mined and quarried in remote locations in the Eastern Desert for use throughout the Roman Empire. The often brutal labor required to harvest these resources was supplied mainly by peasant peoples forced to work by the Romans. This was the so-called corvée system of labor that other later occupiers of Egypt also used. Rome also placed a huge tax burden on the people of Egypt. Not surprisingly, Egyptians came to despise the Roman occupation.

There were also religious conflicts between many Egyptians and their Roman overlords. Christianity came early to Egypt from Palestine and won many converts. For the first three centuries A.D., Christianity was officially rejected by Rome, and at some times Romans carried out vicious persecutions of Christians. Some devout men fled to the desert to pray in isolation and avoid Roman persecution. Among them were St. Paul and St. Anthony, who lived in caves in the northern Eastern Desert. Word of their spiritual strength in an environment of hardship and isolation inspired other pious men. They took up residence in nearby cells, or caves, and occasionally congregated together. This was the beginning of monasticism, which developed fully in the Nile Valley and Western Desert oases in the centuries that followed.

The Roman Emperor Constantine converted to Christianity and declared it the official religion of the Roman Empire in 312 A.D., bringing an end to the persecution of Christians. Constantine moved the capital of his empire from Rome to Byzantium, which was renamed Constantinople (known today as Istanbul, Turkey). His form of Christianity, known as Byzantine and later as Orthodox Christianity, was Egypt's official faith. It was often uncompromising, and it is a sad legacy of that church that it set about defacing and destroying many of the "heathen" monuments of ancient Egypt. There were also differences in religious doctrine between the Byzantine church and the form of Christianity practiced by most Egyptians. In 451 A.D., there was an official split between the Byzantine Church and the Coptic Orthodox Church that was Egypt's own. To this day, most Egyptian Christians are Copts, or Coptic Christians. The Greek Orthodox Church—the successor to Byzantine Orthodoxy—also has followers, including the monks of Sinai's Monastery of St. Katherine.

In 641 A.D. a new faith and way of life swept into Egypt from the Arabian Peninsula. This was Islam. Its followers, called Muslims, practiced a religion revealed to their prophet Muhammad just a few decades earlier. This faith is described in the next chapter. The Muslim army easily defeated the Byzantine forces defending Egypt and settled in for a rather peaceful and tolerant administration of the country. The Arabic-speaking Muslims did little to try to convert the local Coptic Christians and allowed them to run most of their own affairs in their own, mainly Greek, languages. Gradually more and more Egyptians converted to Islam and adopted the Arabic tongue as their own.

For most of the following 200 years Egypt was a province of the greater Muslim Abbasid caliphate, based in Baghdad (modern Iraq). The *caliphs* taxed, but otherwise neglected, Egypt. They found themselves unable to rule it effectively and appointed control of Egypt and other provinces to Turkish military officers. One of these Turkish generals, Ahmad Ibn Tulun, briefly made Egypt independent of Baghdad around 870 A.D. His successors were not as strong, and Baghdad once again reasserted control. But in 969 A.D. a new Muslim power invaded from the west and took control away from the Abbasids. These were the Fatimids, whose base was in Tunisia. Unlike most Egyptians, they were Shi'ite rather than Sunni Muslims, believing that the prophet Muhammad's successors, the caliphs, should have been his blood-relatives rather than elected officials. With one notable exception, however, Fatimid rulers were tolerant of the country's Sunni Muslims, as well as its Christians and Jews. Although there had been ancient Egyptian, Roman, and Byzantine settlements in the area, the Fatimids are credited with founding the city of Cairo. Its Arabic name, al-Qahira, means "The Victorious City." They encouraged and grew wealthy from regional trade, and Egypt again enjoyed prosperity.

The Fatimids were the last Arabs to rule Egypt for almost a thousand years. In 1171 a Kurdish general from Syria named Salah al-Din (or Saladin) brought an end to the Fatimids. He built his own dynasty, called the Ayyubid, and extended his control over Palestine. With Palestine came Jerusalem, and European Christians intent on regaining its holy places waged a war, one of the Crusades, against Saladin. Ayyubid control of Egypt continued until about 1250. By then, the Ayyubids had come to rely for their power on a class of Turkish soldiers called Mameluks. Officially they were slaves, but they had so much power that they killed the last Ayyubid ruler of Egypt and seized control of the country for themselves. They also fought off the Crusaders from Palestine and succeeded in capturing Syria. Mameluk sultans ruled Egypt until 1516, and the country might have

Around 1250 B.C.E., Pharaoh Ramses II commissioned the building of this temple at Abu Simbel on the Nile in southern Egypt. It was probably intended to warn any would-be invaders from further south that they had better not take action against powerful Egypt.

enjoyed progress and prosperity but for the ravages of the plague (the Black Death) during the mid-14th century.

In 1516 Egypt fell to the Ottoman Turks, who ruled from Istanbul. Their empire included much of the eastern Mediterranean region and the Arabian Peninsula and was too large to be governed effectively by their available manpower. The Ottomans thus chose to incorporate the Mameluks into their administration of Egypt. Ottoman control of Egypt was never really strong, and the Mameluks reasserted themselves in an environment of growing civil conflict. Egypt was a tempting target for another strong invader.

Egypt's modern history effectively began in 1798, when French forces under the leadership of Napoleon Bonaparte occupied the country. This began a period of European colonial influence and rule over Egypt that greatly changed the country's orientation and priorities.

France's main interest was in Egypt's strategic location. At the time, France and Great Britain were enemies, and each was trying to increase its economic and political power at the expense of the other. France saw control over Egypt as a way to intervene in Britain's ability to rule supreme over the land and water routes between Europe and India. French forces met only minimal resistance from Egypt's military and settled in for a brief (three year) but influential occupation of Egypt. Napoleon dispatched a large team of scholars to Egypt to study and record the country's rich archaeological, natural, historical, and living human heritage. These so-called savants produced an extraordinary multivolume document called *Description de l'Egypte*. They began the science of Egyptology, which has since brought so much of Egypt's rich archaeological past to life.

It was also during the French occupation that the Rosetta stone was discovered in the Nile Delta. It contained a single official document written in three languages, one of which, Greek, was known to the French, but also the ancient Egypt language, which up until then had not been decipherable. With the Rosetta stone, the French scholar Jean-François Champollion was unable to unlock the mysteries of the ancient language, and suddenly the modern world could make sense of the treasure trove of written documents and stone inscriptions left by the ancients. Another important legacy of the short French occupation of Egypt was the adoption of French as a second language among educated Egyptians. Even today, the

In 969 A.D. the Fatimids, Shi'ite Muslims from Tunisia, founded the city of Cairo. This is one of the remaining ancient gates to the Fatimid city.

most educated Egyptians are raised speaking Arabic, English, and French.

Great Britain ended French control over Egypt in a decisive naval battle near Alexandria. For about the next 75 years, Egypt had some degree of independence from outside powers. A strong ruler named Muhammad Ali, while actually a non-Egyptian (Albanian), struggled to distance the country from its Ottoman Turkish orientation. He wanted to make Egypt an important economic and political power in its own right. A cornerstone of his effort was to make Egypt an important producer of cotton, which was an important global commodity and therefore could help make Egypt wealthy. His agricultural experts and engineers brought Sudanese long staple cotton to Egypt—the same type that is now famous around the world as Egyptian cotton—and began building barrages that would allow this crop to be irrigated in the Nile Delta during the summer (see chapter 2). In the decades following Muhammad Ali's death in 1849, his grandson and successor Ismail tried to make Egypt a more industrialized country. For example, Egyptians built paper processing mills, railways, and modern public works. He also worked with French experts to under-take the building of one of the world's most important waterways, the Suez Canal, which opened for traffic in 1869. Unfortunately, Ismail inherited a burden of debt to European lenders that he paid off in large part by selling ownership of the Suez Canal to Great Britain and France.

Great Britain established itself as Egypt's colonial master in 1882. Egypt assumed the typical colonial role of providing raw materials—particularly cotton—to the mother country, while Great Britain sold finished products back to Egypt. This relationship was more profitable to Britain than to Egypt, and within Egypt there was resentment and sometimes violence against British rule. Great Britain maintained a firm grip on Egypt during World War I, as it joined France in decisively defeating the Ottoman Turks, who had sided with Germany during the war. With the end of the war in 1918 came the end of the life of the "Sick Man of Europe," as the Ottoman Empire was known. Britain and France carved up the Ottoman Lands of the Middle East among themselves, with Britain controlling a swath from Egypt through Palestine (modern Israel) into Iraq.

Great Britain yielded to increasing postwar demands by Egyptians that they should rule themselves and granted independence to Egypt in 1922. In many ways, however, it was independence in name only, and British influence remained strong in Egypt for the next three decades. During this time Egypt became a monarchy ruled by a pro-European king. The last king, Farouk, was ousted in a rebellion of army officers in 1952. That coup d'etat was officially led by a man named Muhammad Neguib, but he was really a figurehead. The power behind the revolt was concentrated in the hands of a young officer named Gamal Abdel Nasser.

Nasser came to power officially in 1956, and over a period of 15 years he had a powerful impact on Egypt's society and its place in the world. He directed what many called a "revolution," appealing to the common man by breaking up the large land holdings of Egypt's wealthy elite and redistributing them as smaller parcels to peasants. He aspired to be a leader for all of the Arab countries by spearheading a 1967 military confrontation with their common enemy, Israel. The results were disastrous for Egypt, as described in chapter 5, but he was successful in wresting the Suez Canal from foreign control. He situated Egypt firmly in the orbit of the Soviet Union, but only after trying to steer a course away from loyalty to either of the great powers. Although he was not always successful in his efforts, Nasser did instill in Egyptians a new confidence about themselves and a new sense of solidarity and independence.

Anwar Sadat, who became president of Egypt upon Nasser's death in 1971, reversed the country's direction and sought strong ties with the West, especially the United States.

Completed in 1869, the Suez Canal is one of the world's most strategic waterways. The canal has been a focus of many Middle Eastern Wars. Today the spot is a popular day-trip destination for the people of Cairo.

He launched a new war against Israel in 1973, this one more successful than the 1967 conflict, but then made Egypt the first Arab country to sign a peace treaty with Israel (see chapter 5). His assassination in 1981, carried out in protest over that treaty, brought his vice president Hosni Mubarak to power. President Mubarak continued down Sadat's pathway of firm ties with the West and expanded Egypt's role as regional peacemaker. Some of his historic problems and opportunities are described in chapter 5. He brought Egypt into the third millennium, a time of great challenge for the country and the region.

The minarets of the al-Azhar University, founded in Cairo in 969 A.D., are shown here. The university is still an Islamic educational facility.

# 4

# People and Culture

E gypt enjoys worldwide fame for its wealth of ancient artifacts. Although less well known, its living cultures are also very rich, and this chapter will introduce the modern people and ways of life in Egypt.

Egypt is overwhelmingly an Arab country, meaning that most of its people speak Arabic as their native language. Arabic originated in and around the Arabian Peninsula and is in the Semitic family of languages that includes Hebrew, spoken by Jews in the world today, and Aramaic, the language used by Jesus. Arabic speakers settled in Egypt at different times, but one of the most important migrations was when Muslim Arabs came to Egypt bearing their new faith in 641 A.D.

There are several religious minorities in Egypt, the most important being the Coptic Christians who make up about 6 percent of the population, but Egypt is overwhelmingly a Muslim country—about

94 percent of Egyptians practice Islam. Many Muslims around the world look to Egypt for religious inspiration and instruction. One of the world's leading centers of Islamic learning is al-Azhar University, founded in 969 A.D. by the Fatimids when they established the city of Cairo. The clerics of al-Azhar are, like most Egyptians, Sunni or orthodox Muslims who practice a "moderate" form of Islam with little concern for politics or revolt. There are, however, more militant Muslims, and their struggle with the government of Egypt is described in the next chapter.

As a visitor to Egypt, one of the most noticeable things is how devout the Egyptians are and how deeply their faith penetrates every part of their lives. Every city and town has a skyline that includes domes and minarets (towers), the characteristic architectural forms of the mosques where Muslims worship. Five times daily, including at the crack of dawn, a call to prayer issues forth from the minarets. Muslims may go to the mosque to pray, and most do on Friday, the Muslim holy day, or they may pray in their homes, offices, or along the street. Prayer is one of the five pillars, or requirements, of Islam. The others are the profession of faith, which requires Muslims to recognize that there is only one God, called *Allah* in Arabic, and that the prophet Muhammad is God's messenger; to give alms or charity to the poor; to fast (abstain from food and drinks) from dawn to sunset during the month of Ramadan; and performing the pilgimage (*hajj*) to the Saudi Arabian city of Mecca if one is physically and financially able.

Another feature that might impress a first time visitor to Egypt is how many Egyptians there are. Egypt is a populous country, among the top three in the Middle East. With its 70 million people, only Iran and Turkey, each of which also has about 70 million, rival it. All but about 5 percent of Egyptians live on the narrow ribbon of the Nile Valley and in the Nile Delta, so the impressions of overpopulation and crowding are strong.

Until recently, Egypt's population growth was so rapid

Egyptians have a strong sense of family. The children, who are beloved, are expected to work and contribute to the household finances.

that it was considered explosive. Many social scientists warned that there was a population "bomb" that would explode in Egypt, resulting in poverty, hunger, famine, epidemic, or warfare. The population rocketed from 2.5 million in the early 1800s to about 10 million in 1900, 20 million in 1950, 40 million in 1980, and 70 million in 2002. The growth occurred because of falling death rates, meaning fewer children died and people generally lived longer because of better food production and distribution, and because medical care and technologies improved. At the same time birth rates remained high. Egypt is like most of the world's other developing countries in that parents often believe that having more children will actually help them lead more prosperous lives. For example, more children mean more hands to work in the fields in rural areas, or to work in a clothing factory or an automobile mechanic shop in the cities. There are no laws against child labor in Egypt. This point of view is probably different from that of American parents, who are more likely to believe that if they have fewer children the family will be more prosperous.

Around the world there is clear evidence that the wealthier the parents are, and the more education they have, the fewer children they will have. This correlation has been proving true even in Egypt in recent years. Egypt's level of education has risen in the past few decades, and at the same time, the birth rate—a reflection of how many children Egyptians are choosing to have—has been falling. So, while Egypt's population is very large and is growing, the rate of growth has slowed a lot. Back in 1985, Egypt's annual rate of population growth was 2.7 percent. At that rate, the country's population would have doubled in 27 years. In 2001, the population growth rate was 2.1 percent; at that rate, the country's population would double in 34 years. This is an improvement in a land whose agricultural and other resources are limited. But the sheer number of people added to the population every year is of much concern—there were 23 million more Egyptians—a staggering 50 percent more—in 2001 than in 1985.

Another characteristic of Egypt's people is how young they are—how many infants, children, and young adults there are among the population. It is not a mistaken impression. More than one third—36%—of Egyptians are under the age of 15.

Finally, a visitor's impression of Egypt's population might be one of surprise that so many people live in cities—Westerners might have had an image of Egyptians working the land as they did in biblical times. Recently, however, not only have Egypt's cities grown rapidly, but their proportion in the overall population has also increased. In 2001, 43 percent of Egyptians were city dwellers (versus about 20 percent in 1910), so the rural people are only a modest majority.

Egypt's rural peasant farmers, called *fellahiin* in Arabic,

A village in the Western Desert's Siwa Oasis. Newer concrete and cinder block buildings, in the distance, are beginning to replace traditional mud brick.

live in some 4,000 villages in the Nile Valley and Nile Delta. The typical village is a densely packed group of mud brick structures built in the midst of the green cultivated area. As in ancient times, Egyptian peasants today build their cemeteries on nearby desert margins, or on unproductive land near the village. The quaint images of men and women in flowing robes and children riding donkeys in these villages lead many outsiders to speak of the timeless or biblical Egyptian village. But the villages are changing: Electric pumps are replacing human or animal powered water lifting techniques, and paved roads, electricity lines, telephones, and televisions have been established in all but the most remote villages.

What has not changed as much as Egyptians would like is the general poverty of the village. Despite land reform since the time of President Nasser, few peasants own more than very small farm plots. There simply is not enough good farmland in the Nile Valley and Nile Delta to go around for the growing population. Nor are there sufficient nonfarming jobs in the countryside. The result is that people flee the countryside to seek jobs in the cities. Social scientists call them "nonselective migrants," people who have been "pushed" off the land because the land cannot support them. Also leaving the villages and going to the cities are the "selective migrants," the most educated and ambitious villagers, who are "pulled" to the city by the near-certainty that they will find productive employment there. In this way they represent what is called a "brain drain," meaning the rural areas will probably stay underdeveloped in part because the people best able to do something about the poverty are leaving these places. Regardless of the push and pull factors that influence their decision to move, in the end they represent more people in the cities. This helps to explain why Egypt has such apparently overcrowded urban areas.

The largest city by far is Cairo, with a population conservatively estimated at 15 million people. It is an urban giant, a megacity, the largest city in Africa and one of the largest in the world. An amazing 20 percent of all Egyptians, and half of the country's urban population, live in Cairo. The second ranking city is Alexandria (about four million), along the Mediterranean coast. Other important cities of the Nile Delta are Tanta and al-Mahalla al-Kubra, and major cities of the Nile Valley are Minya, Asyut, Qena, and Aswan.

Cairo has a clear geographic reason for being Egypt's leading city—it is strategically located near the junction of the Nile Delta and the Nile Valley. It is really several cities established one next to another over time, beginning with the ancient Egyptians, and gradually fused into one flowing whole. The historic heart of the city is in the east, where the Fatimids established walled al-Qahira in 969 A.D. It has all the typical elements of the classic Middle Eastern city, known in Arabic as a *medina*, that is walled for protection. It has monumental places of worship, including many mosques with their distinctive domes and minarets; and it has a sprawling *suq*, or market-place, clearly recognizable as the ancestor of the modern Western shopping mall. And it has a rather chaotic street plan that was not laid out along the Western grid system and was never designed for modern vehicular traffic. Thus the old city has had great new swaths cut into it and elevated highways erected above it to accommodate Cairo's infamous traffic.

A walk though Cairo's *medina* is truly an enchanting, colorful, and noisy walk through time. It can also be a bit disheartening, too, because it is one of the poorer parts of the city. Some people, such as shopkeepers, craftsmen, and taxi drivers, have steady but not well-paying work; and there is a large and poor underclass of beggars and street vendors (people who will, for example, approach a rider in a car to sell a flower necklace or a pack of tissues). The wealthier people tend to live further west in the newer part of the city, or in the suburbs that have cropped up in recent decades on the city's desert edges. Some of these suburbs, such as Zamalek on Gezira Island, are quite affluent. Many diplomats and successful businesspeople live here, and their children attend Egypt's private schools and universities. Their homes and apartments are spacious and well furnished, and they own automobiles. This is in great contrast with the majority of Egyptians, inside and outside the cities, who often live in cramped and deterio-rating quarters and could only dream of having cars and other expensive luxuries.

Cairo's most unique area is the so-called City of the Dead, in the eastern part of the city. It began as flat open space well away from the city and was a logical place to have a cemetery.

Cairo's City of the Dead cemetery is home to refugees with no other place to go. The government has recognized the city and has started to provide public services to the area.

Many of the wealthy Turkish Mameluks were buried in magnificent mausoleums there. Over time, citizens of Cairo established small family burial plots there, and it grew into a sprawling cemetery. The citizenship of the City of the Dead began to change dramatically after Egypt's war with Israel in 1973. That war was centered on the Suez Canal Zone, where many civilians chose to flee their homes in the cities of Port Said, Ismailia, and Suez. They sought safety to the west in Cairo, but there was not sufficient housing for them in apartments. These refugees began to settle in places were there were four walls, though seldom with a roof overhead—the walled cemetery compounds of the City of the Dead. In time, some moved into Cairo's apartments or back to their rebuilt canal cities. But someone new is always arriving in Cairo from some distant town or village, and more people settled in the cemetery. Some eventually put a roof over the compound, then a second story or even a third: Now, while the dead are still buried here, it is mainly a city of the living. Cairo and Egypt's leaders were embarrassed by the impression given of Egyptians forced to live in a graveyard and for a time tried to relocate the inhabitants. But there was not enough money to build new quarters for all these squatters, and the authorities finally relented and began to treat the City of the Dead like any other part of Cairo. Today it has most of the services found elsewhere in Cairo, including electricity, running water, telephone lines, and mail.

Northeast of the City of the Dead is another of Cairo's unique areas, the quarter of the *zabaaliin*, or trash collectors. They are Coptic Christians that have collected and sorted Cairo's trash for generations. As most Cairenes (residents of Cairo) sleep, the zabaaliin cover almost every nook and cranny of the city collecting the waste in straw baskets. They load the trash onto a donkey-pulled cart in the street and by daybreak return to their base. Here they begin sorting the waste: Paper, plastic, glass, metal, and other materials are separated into various piles, and organic waste is directed to a giant compost heap. Very little of this waste actually ends up as waste. Most of it is recycled so that, for example, you may buy a bag of peanuts in which the bag is a rather clean sheet of paper on which a student did homework a few days earlier. The recycling is profitable for the zabaaliin. Although their part of the city has giant mounds of refuse, the people are not poor,

Coptic Christians have collected trash in Egypt for centuries. Here, the children of the *zabaaliin* (trash collectors) sort through trash for recycling.

and they have come far with their enterprise. Recently they won an official contract to collect Cairo's waste, beating bids for more modern, motorized Western-style collection systems. And they won a prestigious United Nations environmental award that recognized the Earth-friendliness of their labors.

To the Westerner accustomed to the potential dangers of

urban life, especially violent crime, perhaps the most surprising thing about the Egyptian city is the overwhelming sense of security. Violence is almost unknown, and even petty theft is rare. Sometimes a pickpocket will take advantage of the over-crowding on a bus and lift a wallet, but that is about it. A foreigner can walk day or night in any part of Cairo, even its poorest quarters, and not fear for his or her safety. More likely than not, the visitor will be greeted repeatedly by the locals: "Hello, where are you from? Come, come, have tea, meet my family." Hospitality and generosity are important traits in the Arab culture, and perhaps no Arabs are friendlier than the Egyptians. That tradition of kindness, as well as their deep religious beliefs, probably has a lot to do with Egypt's low crime rate.

Yet another culture associated with hospitality is found in Egypt, but far from the big cities and the villages of the Nile Valley. In the deserts live the Bedouin, Arabic-speaking pastoral nomads that came to Egypt from the Arabian Peninsula many centuries ago. They are called pastoral nomads because they keep livestock—animals such as sheep, goats, and camels that feed on pasture—and because they must move about the desert to find places where there has been rain and therefore there are growing plants for the animals to feed on. Their way of life is about 10,000 years old. It emerged in the Middle East not long after people domesticated plants and animals and began farming, and it preceded the urban way of life by perhaps 5,000 years. The Bedouin livelihood can be difficult. Sometimes there are long droughts that make it difficult to keep livestock healthy. And sleeping out under the stars or in a wool tent, never having a house or a village to call home, can be a challenge; there are none of the modern conveniences of life, and there is no medical care in the wilderness. But the Bedouin pride themselves on the freedom their migratory way of life brings them. Traditionally, they have not had to pay taxes, to serve in the military, or to perform forced labor like many of their village-dwelling counterparts did.

Before about the middle of the 20th century, villagers, pastoral nomads, and urbanites were part of a framework of trade relationships that was generally beneficial to all. A geographer called these relationships the "ecological trilogy." The village peasant farmers were the cornerstone of the trilogy. They grew the cereal grains, fruits, and vegetables that fed city people. Desert pastoral nomads also ate farmers' produce, buying flour, for example, when they visited towns periodically to sell their livestock. Villagers benefited in that exchange because they often lacked enough land to support animals like sheep and goats, and by trading with the Bedouin they could get these animals' meat, hide, horn, milk, wool, and bone. City people, too, gave something back to the villagers in the form of education, trained medical providers and equipment, and entertainment such as music.

These relationships continue, but they are not as clearly defined or recognizable as before. Most of Egypt's Bedouin have settled down (in a process called sedentarization) and have effectively dropped out of the trilogy; only in the Eastern Desert are there still traditional nomads. They have chosen to settle, generally because they have been tempted by the more reliable and profitable work available to them as wage laborers; for example, they are often mechanics, guards, and guides in desert towns. Most live in fixed dwellings in or near the desert towns. The family still keeps some animals, but usually only a few, not the 40 or 50 sheep and goats they used to have in the wilderness.

Even though their ways of life have changed, all of these people still call themselves Bedouin, and they still affiliate with the tribe more than with any other unit—Ma'aza tribespeople, for example, call themselves Ma'aza and do not really think of themselves as Egyptian. To be a member of a tribe means to have descended from a single, common male ancestor who lived many generations ago. A tribesperson almost always marries within the tribe—it is frowned upon to do otherwise.

This 'Ababda Bedouin of the Eastern Desert continues to maintain the lifestyle of the desert nomad.

In the desert the tribes have separate areas in which pasture, water sources, and game animals belong to them. Traditionally one tribe has always shared its resources with others, knowing that it too may need to call on those others in a time of drought or other environmental stress.

This concludes the introduction to Egypt's population, cultures, and settlements, but there is more on the daily lives of Egyptians in Chapter 7.

The hydroelectric station of the Aswan High Dam is shown here. The United States withdrew its offer of financing to build the dam because of President Nasser's hesitancy to accept the conditions of a loan.

# 5

# Government

S ince the 1952 revolution when Egypt threw off the colonial yoke and was truly free, this Arab giant has walked a tightrope in the international arena: between the superpowers, between the Arab East and the West, between secular and religious affairs within the country, and between confrontation and accommodation with its 20th-century foe, Israel. The political challenges have been huge and the choices difficult. Egypt's leaders have been invested with the authority to back up their decisions.

## The International Arena

When Gamal Abdel Nasser became president in 1956, he resolved to make Egypt an important and independent power both in the region and among developing nations around the world. He called for "nonalignment," meaning that Egypt should not be subservient to the needs of either of the world's superpowers, the United States and the Soviet Union. He was also a spokesman for Arab nationalism, a movement that would bring together Arab nations as a collective counterweight against great power and Israeli interests in the region. To this end, Egypt was briefly unified with Syria as a single country called the United Arab Republic. Nasser found nonalignment difficult. Egypt needed a lot of money to build the Aswan High Dam and effectively had to choose between seeking money from the West or from the Soviet Union. Nasser chose the West, asking the United States and Great Britain for the necessary funds. Those countries responded with loan conditions that Nasser thought would hurt his standing as an independent, nonaligned leader. So, for many months he did not accept or reject the Western loan offer. By the time he finally did agree to its terms, the Western lenders, especially the United States, were so angry with Nasser that they withdrew the offer.

Momentous events followed. Nasser nationalized the Suez Canal, meaning that he took control of it away from the British and French and placed it in Egyptian hands. The money Egypt earned by charging tolls on ships passing through the canal would be used to pay for the construction of the Aswan High Dam, according to Nasser. Egypt also sought funding and technical assistance for the dam from the Soviet Union, and for the following 15 years Soviet influence in Egypt was very strong. Great Britain and France decided to confront Egypt militarily and sent troops into the Suez Canal Zone. Israeli forces also participated in the 1956 war against Egypt, especially to destroy Soviet weapons in the Sinai Peninsula that could be used against Israel. Within days the three invading powers held the Sinai Peninsula and the Suez Canal. However, there was strong international condemnation of these military actions, particularly by the United States, and Britain, France, and Israel soon withdrew. The Suez Canal was now firmly and finally Egyptian, a great victory for the nationalist Nasser.

The next war did not go Nasser's way. In 1967, Egypt received faulty intelligence information from the Soviet Union, indicating that Israeli troops were poised for an invasion of Syria. Egypt warned its Syrian ally of the threat, and declared the Gulf of Aqaba off-limits to Israeli shipping. Nasser also called for United Nations peacekeeping troops to leave Sinai, where they had been stationed since the 1956 war. Israeli leaders read all of these actions as signs that Arab neighbors were about to attack and decided to strike first. Israeli warplanes took to the skies on June 5, 1967, quickly destroying the Egyptian and Syrian air forces on their respective runways. Having established what military commanders call air superiority, Israeli forces also advanced rapidly on the ground. Within six days, Israeli troops captured all of the Sinai Peninsula, right up to the Suez Canal; the Gaza Strip, a sliver of land that had been controlled by Egypt since 1948 and had a large Palestinian population; the Golan Heights, a Syrian highland region that overlooked northeastern Israel; and the West Bank, that part of Jordan that lay west of the Jordan River, where the population was mostly Palestinian Arab. Israel's capture of the West Bank also included the prize catch of the Old City of Jerusalem, which contains Judaism's holiest site—the Western Wall—as well as places sacred to Muslims and Christians. Now humiliated and defeated, Nasser tried to step down as Egypt's leader, but the public rallied behind him and he remained in office until his death in 1970.

Nasser was succeeded by his vice president, another officer from the 1952 coup, Anwar Sadat. President Sadat was widely predicted to be an inconsequential Egyptian leader, but he defied the expectations with some bold and risky political steps. First, he expelled the Soviets from Egypt, severed the country's relationship with its Communist benefactor, and began seeking stronger ties with the West, particularly the United States. Second, he decided to shake up the stalemated political landscape of the Middle East by joining Syria in a surprise attack

The summit of Sinai's Jebel Musa (top center) is the site where, according to Judeo-Christian tradition, God gave the Ten Commandments to Moses. At the base of the mountain is the sixth century Monastery of St. Katherine.

against Israel in October 1973. Egyptian forces made remarkable progress against strong Israeli defenses east of the Suez Canal and pushed well into the Sinai Peninsula. These gains were soon reversed as Israeli troops encircled and cut off the Egyptian army within Sinai. A ceasefire was declared. Egypt did not regain the Sinai Peninsula but declared at least a moral victory for taking on and not losing to Israel. And Egypt did get a solid gain out of the conflict—renewed control of the Suez Canal, which had been closed to shipping since the 1967 war. Egypt now had a sorely needed source of money.

Sadat's last bold, risky step was peacemaking with Israel. He decided to overcome the longstanding regional policy that no Arab nation should accept Israel's right to exist. In 1977 he flew to Israel, and television viewers around the world witnessed his historic handshake with Israel's Prime Minister Menachem Begin and other leaders. Within two years, Sadat, Begin, and

U.S. President Jimmy Carter concluded an extraordinary agreement called the Camp David Accord (because it was negotiated at the U.S. presidential retreat of Camp David, Maryland). It was the first "land for peace" deal between Israel and an Arab neighbor, meaning Israel gave back some of the Arab land it had occupied in 1967 in exchange for peaceful relations with the Arab country. In this case, Israel gave the Sinai Peninsula back to Egypt. There were handsome financial rewards for Sadat's peacemaking. Egypt now once again controlled its Sinai oilfields and the potential tourism development sites of the Sinai coasts. The United States began giving Egypt about two billion dollars in aid every year, a contribution that continues today and that is second only to Israel's aid package of about three billion dollars yearly. Egypt had now become a firmly pro-Western, "moderate" Arab country.

But the peacemaking also cost Sadat, and to some extent Egypt, dearly. Egypt had been the figurative center of the Arab world and the headquarters of its diplomatic bloc, the Arab League. As punishment for Egypt's treaty with Israel, the Arab League expelled Egypt and relocated its headquarters, and most Arab countries broke diplomatic ties with Egypt. Within the country there was little heartfelt warmth about the treaty with Israel, and a state of "cold peace" settled in between the countries. Some Egyptians, particularly those who advocated a radical form of Islam as an alternative to Egypt's secular politics, denounced Sadat as an un-Islamic traitor that had sold out to Israel and the West. One such faction, Islamic Jihad, succeeded in assassinating President Sadat at a military parade in Cairo on October 6, 1981. He was succeeded by his vice president, Hosni Mubarak, who was still in office when this book went to press in 2002.

## Domestic Affairs

Egypt is officially a democracy, but its citizens enjoy few of the democratic freedoms and representation found in Western democracies, and Egypt's political system is usually described as authoritarian. There is a president (now Hosni Mubarak) that is nominated by the parliament, which is called the People's Assembly. Following the nomination, the president is elected for a six-year term in a popular referendum; the Egyptian people are essentially asked to answer "yes" or "no" to the question: "Do you want this man to be your president?" Every six years, the answer is a resounding "yes," typically around 95 percent. There are many questions about how well the reported result reflects real feelings among Egyptians, and there are larger questions about Egypt's democratic process. Mubarak has been repeatedly nominated president by his party, the National Democratic Party, whose overwhelming grip on power within the Parliament (holding about 95 percent of the seats) often seems to come about through suspect ways. Recent parliamentary elections have been accompanied by widespread voter fraud, including the stuffing of some ballot boxes and the suspicious disappearance of others, and the arrest and harassment of opposition supporters just prior to elections. Leading intellectuals have been jailed for encouraging Egyptians to vote for opposition candidates— and even simply for encouraging them to vote. Sometimes opposition candidates have boycotted the elections to express their unhappiness with the political system.

There are legitimate opposition parties in Egypt, but they are not allowed to gain much strength and threaten the seat of power. The New Wafd party is the largest of these. Its members, including Coptic Christians, businessmen, former military officers, Islamists, and onetime supporters of President Nasser, are mainly from the middle and upper classes. Another opposition party is the Socialist Labor Party, which has many members that support the development of a more Islamic way of governing Egypt. There is also a mainly Marxist party called the National Progressive Unionist Grouping.

President Mubarak can appoint a vice president, but it is a telling indication of Egypt's authoritarian political system that he never has. Ever since he came to office with the assassination

This Muslim man fulfills his duty to pray by taking time for prayer on a Cairo rooftop. Prayer is one of the five pillars of Islam.

of President Sadat in 1981, Mubarak has ruled Egypt with emergency powers granted to him by the Parliament. These powers suspend many of the freedoms that typically exist in a democracy and are justified on the grounds of maintaining security within the country. Real threats to that security, and certainly to the Mubarak regime, do exist, and most of them are in the form of Islamist opposition. That opposition has been Egypt's most serious political problem since about 1980.

A careful distinction must be made between *Islamic* and *Islamists*. Most Egyptians are Muslims who lead an Islamic way of life. They observe the five pillars of the faith, practice acts of kindness, and generally feeling tolerant of other faiths and ways of life. But they also believe that the country and society should be organized along secular, rather than religious, lines. There are a small number of Muslims within Egypt who are Islamists. Their slogan is "Islam is the answer," meaning that all of the country's and society's problems, particularly poverty and the lack of political participation, can be solved by adopting Islamic law as the law of the land and substituting religious for secular institutions at most levels. There is a wide range of Islamist opinions and organizations in Egypt, but their fundamental message is that the current government is politically illegitimate, too pro-Western, too accommodating to Israel, and not sufficiently Islamic, and should therefore be replaced.

The oldest and largest of the estimated 30 to 60 Islamist movements in Egypt is the Muslim Brotherhood, founded in 1928. The organization made an attempt on the life of President Nasser, and he cracked down on it. President Sadat allowed the Muslim Brotherhood more freedom, and the movement continued to gain support during the Mubarak years. The breadth of this support is difficult to estimate, especially since the government will not allow the movement to form a political party. It is a mainstream and moderate movement, especially when compared with some of Egypt's other Islamist groups. These include Islamic Jihad, which assassinated President Sadat in retaliation for his peacemaking with Israel, and the al-Gami'at al-Islamiyya (Islamic Group), which carried out a series of attacks on foreign tourists in Egypt in the 1990s. In striking at Egypt's vital tourist industry, these militants hoped to destabilize and perhaps cause the downfall of the Mubarak regime. Millions of Egyptians depend economically in some way on tourism. For this reason, the Islamic Group lost much popular sympathy when it carried out a gruesome assault on foreign tourists at an ancient Egyptian temple in Luxor in 1997, in which 58 were killed. Prior to that, Egypt's Islamists had enjoyed growing public support by coming faithfully to the aid of Egyptians in need—in the wake of the 1992 earthquake in Cairo, for example—while government emergency services seemed slow and reluctant to take action.

There are some strong links between these militant Islamist organizations in Egypt and the events leading up to and following the attacks on New York City and Washington, D.C., in

September 2001. Ayman al-Zawahiri, the one-time physician who became the right hand man of Osama bin Laden in the al-Qaida organization, was jailed for his role in the Islamic Jihad's assassination of President Sadat. Islamic Jihad's spiritual leader, a blind cleric named Omar Abd al-Rahman, was convicted and imprisoned in the United States for involvement in the first attack on New York's World Trade Center, in 1993. These men are indications that to some extent Egypt was successful in exporting its Islamist problem abroad, by deporting the militant leaders or allowing them to relocate. As early as the 1980s, some went to Afghanistan to join the ranks of the "Afghan Arabs" that helped locals to fight and eventually expel the Soviet invaders of Afghanistan. The Islamist victory against a powerful enemy gave much confidence to the fighters, and in time they sought more ambitious targets and recruited more followers, especially from Egypt. In the political vacuum that followed the Soviet withdrawal, Afghanistan became a kind of haven for Islamist militants training to overthrow their main enemies: the autocratic governments of the Middle East, including Egypt and Saudi Arabia; the country of Israel; and the United States, the nation that had since 1990 stationed troops in Islam's holy land of Saudi Arabia.

Egypt has used means other than deportation to deal with its Islamist problem. Since coming to office, President Mubarak has carried out a virtual war against the more militant groups. Egypt has an extraordinary security apparatus, with informants and agents at every level of society. While the militants have carried out successful attacks, many of their efforts have undoubtedly been thwarted by the massive arrests based on information provided by Egyptian security. Human rights groups complain about the state's heavy-handedness against Islamist suspects, and there are widespread reports of torture, along with the routine detention in jail without speedy trial. When legal action finally comes it is often severe; scores of convicted Islamists have been executed in Mubarak's Egypt. The country's reputation for human rights and civil liberties is generally poor. This is in part because of government restrictions on freedom of the press. But the government also makes it very difficult for nongovernmental organizations (NGOs)—including human rights and other "watchdog" groups—to be formed.

Egypt has one of the world's oldest, largest, and perhaps most inefficient government bureaucracies. The government provides numerous services, but often of poor quality. The country is only gradually changing from a mainly socialist state—in which the government owns and operates most businesses and services—to a mostly capitalist state in which private institutions perform all but the essential national functions. There is more about the economic aspects of Egypt's transformation from socialism to capitalism in the following chapter.

Egypt's government has an agreement with its people: It will take care of them. It tries to be a welfare state by promising every Egyptian that no matter what else is going on in the country or abroad, the government will try to help feed, clothe, and house its people. It also will provide for their medical needs, produce in factories what they need to consume, educate them (even college tuition is free at the public universities), guarantee them work in the government if they get college degrees, and help transport them to work. In this contract with the people, the government wants to ensure that Egyptians are not denied social services and that there will never be hunger, starvation, epidemic, or widespread illiteracy. To some extent the system is successful. Egypt does not have famines, for example, and indices of quality of life such as literacy and life expectancy are better now than they were before the 1952 revolution. The poorest people have been able to afford the basic necessities of life, especially staple food items. And students that complete their college degrees do get jobs.

The problem is that the contract between government and people is not fulfilled very effectively. Although the prices of some basic food items are kept artificially low so

Cairo's *medina*, once its vibrant heart, is a poor and neglected section of the city today.

that poor people can buy them, they are still relatively expensive. The medical care is often bad—equipment is broken or outdated, and the best doctors may be found only in private practice, where their fees are too high for most people to afford. College graduates do get jobs, but typically they join the ranks of millions of other employees jammed into already bloated government offices where there is little work to do and there are few rewards for doing work—the salaries are very low. Visitors to Egypt would almost certainly have at least one experience dealing with the government bureaucracy. A simple piece of paperwork—like extending a tourist

The Egyptian word for bread is *'aysh*, meaning "life." The government would like to reduce the amount of money it spends to keep bread affordable for Egypt's poor, but this has proven to be politically risky.

visa to stay in the country—would lead the visitor through an incredibly complex and time-consuming series of visits to different offices within the giant *Mugamma* building in downtown Cairo where people would look over and put stamps on the application. It might seem that few of the people in these offices are doing any serious work, and most are sitting idly, drinking tea, or conversing. It is not a mistaken impression. The system is not supposed to work efficiently because if it did, there would not be work for many of these people. There is an old saying about the socialist system in the old Soviet Union that applies well to the Egyptian government employees: "The government pretends to pay us, and we pretend to work." This kind of experience in Egypt can be frustrating for both the person seeking help and the office workers. But do not forget that the United States also has a formidable bureaucracy—think about filing income tax, or what an Egyptian has to go through to get a visa to visit the United States.

The development of desert cities could relieve much of the pressure on services in Cairo and other Egyptian cities, but Egyptians have not embraced these new settlements.

# The Economy

E gypt is a poor country that wants desperately to become more industrialized and wealthy but is finding it difficult to do so because of its growing population, a shortage or natural resources, and management problems. It is not among the world's poorest countries, like many of those to the south in Africa, nor is it among the rather well-to-do developing countries such as Malaysia and South Korea. It is in the middle ranks of less developed countries. A reliable measure of its wealth ($3,460 on the gross national income purchasing power parity per capita scale) puts it on about the same standard of living as Morocco, Guatemala, Jamaica, and China. Fully half of Egypt's people are classified officially as poor, with 40 percent in the middle class, and 10 percent wealthy.

Egypt is not an important manufacturing country on the world stage—it is not a major exporter of brand name consumer electronics and automobiles or industrial components like iron and steel. Its main sources of revenue are from international tourism, oil exports, the transit fees charged to ships passing through the Suez Canal, and the money sent home by Egyptians working abroad. Each of these deserves a closer look.

Tourism is sometimes Egypt's most valuable source of foreign currency—the "hard" money it needs because its own currency, the Egyptian pound (E£), is not convertible outside Egypt. Tourism is also a vulnerable industry for Egypt—thus the qualification that it is "sometimes" number one. The country has tremendous tourist attractions: the pyramids and other magnificent monuments of ancient Egypt, the tranquility and romance of the Nile River, the impressive wilderness mountains of Sinai, the rich coral reefs lying off of sun-baked beaches, and the charm and hospitality of the Egyptians themselves. Tourists have been coming to Egypt for more than 3,000 years, going home to spread the word about the country's wonders.

When foreign travelers believe they are safe, Egypt's tourism has been successful. In the year 2000 tourism brought in $4.3 billion dollars, accounting for 10 percent of Egypt's gross domestic product. More than two million Egyptians have jobs directly related to tourism, and millions more receive some trickle-down benefit from the money foreign tourists spend. But those livelihoods and benefits are unreliable. Whenever there is a terrorist incident in Egypt, in the Middle East, or abroad but with connections to the Middle East, tourism to Egypt drops off. It usually rebounds, but only slowly. The most serious downturn in tourism came after the attacks on the United States in September 2001. In October, tourism was already off by almost 50 percent. That was on top of already steep declines following an escalation of tensions between Israel and Palestinians beginning in August 2000. Following the 2001 attacks, hotels, airlines, and cruise ships cut prices

Egypt exports crude oil and petroleum products, and its economy suffers when the price of oil drops. Most of Egypt's oil is produced from beneath and near the Gulf of Suez.

dramatically and sought more budget-minded tourists, especially from Russia.

Oil is a more reliable resource for Egypt, but it is a finite one (and Egypt has only modest reserves of it) and is also subject to the whims of global events. Most of the country's oil is around and below the waves of the Gulf of Suez, especially along the west coast of the Sinai Peninsula (that is one reason President Sadat wanted to win back the peninsula from Israel). Egypt is not a member of the Organization of Petroleum Exporting Countries (OPEC), the 12-nation member cartel that has the biggest role in deciding global production and pricing of oil. But like the OPEC members, Egypt benefits when the price of oil is reasonably high and suffers when the price declines. Egypt had an especially bad budget situation in the late 1980s, when the price of oil sank to as low as $9 per barrel. It was doing well in 2000 when the price was around $30 per barrel. But then the terrorist attacks on the United States sent many economies around the world into recession. Industrial production slowed down, meaning less oil was needed. So the price of oil fell, and Egypt saw less revenue.

Not as profitable as oil, but a steadier source of income, is the fee Egypt charges to each ship passing through the Suez Canal. Oil tankers once made up the most important traffic through the Canal. When fighting between Egypt and Israel closed the canal in 1973, however, a new generation of super-tankers was built to carry Middle Eastern oil by sea around Africa to Western Europe and North America. When the canal reopened in 1975, it was not wide and deep enough to accommodate these huge vessels. Egypt is now enlarging the canal to take in those ships.

Remittances, or money earned by Egyptians working abroad and then carried or sent home to Egypt where it is spent, is the last of Egypt's four main revenue earners. This source of income is a mixed blessing for the country. On the one hand, it represents an international "brain drain." Some of the best and brightest Egyptian engineers and doctors, for example, are working abroad and therefore not helping their country to develop at home. On the other hand, Egypt simply does not have enough jobs available, or sufficiently attractive salaries for these professionals to begin with, so it encourages this kind of work. The oil-wealthy countries of the Persian Gulf, such as Saudi Arabia, Kuwait, and the United Arab Emirates, employ most of the skilled and unskilled Egyptian workers. Their salaries are usually much higher than they would be in Egypt, and when they come home they have not only cash in their pockets but typically mounds of consumer electronics and other luxuries purchased in the Gulf States.

There is also considerable foreign aid pouring into Egypt, with the main donors and lenders being the United States and the European Union. The United States provides about $2 billion worth of aid to Egypt each year. Some of this goes toward improving the country's poor infrastructure, including its drinking water and sewage systems. Much, however, is military aid— new fighter jets and other war materiel, for example—that is of little apparent benefit to the Egyptian people. Critics of foreign aid point out that there are many strings attached; for example, the engineering firms hired to build the new sewage facilities are American, so much of the money goes back to the United States. There are also international agencies like the International Monetary Fund (IMF) and World Bank that lend money for Egypt to invest in development projects. It is sometimes difficult for Egypt to keep up with the payments on these loans, and pressure from the lenders forces Egyptian leaders to make difficult and unpopular decisions.

The most famous example of a tough and unpopular decision was President Sadat's 1977 decree that the subsidies on bread and other basic food items should be cut. Subsidies are the monies the government pays to make items available to the public at below-market cost, and they have long been part of the covenant between the state and its people. In 1977, IMF pressure about its own loan to Egypt led Sadat to cut the expensive subsidies. The prices of bread, rice, cooking oil, and other staples shot up immediately by almost 40 percent. Also immediately, Egyptians took to the streets to protest the action. They burned nightclubs, railway cars, and government buildings; they also overturned cars, attacked foreign airline offices, and generally wreaked havoc until, within hours, the government backed down and restored the subsidies. There were some fatalities and many injuries. After the January 1977 food riots, the government has proceeded cautiously in economic reforms that would hurt the poor most.

Around the time of the food riots, President Sadat instituted a new economic policy for Egypt that was meant to improve the country's standard of living and give it some footing on the international economic stage. It was called the *infitah,* meaning opening—Egypt's doors would now be opened to foreign investment. Up to that time, almost all of Egypt's industries were state-run. They produced few export goods and few consumer products that Egyptians wanted to buy. The open door was supposed to change that, inviting international businesses to take advantage of Egypt's abundant and well-trained work force to manufacture products for foreign and local consumption. There has been only modest progress so far. There are consumer goods—almost any convenience of modern life can be purchased in Egypt today—but most are imported. The hoped-for emergence of a dynamic, private manufacturing sector has not taken place. Many foreign businesses are put off by the risks of investing in the volatile Middle East, by the red tape involved in setting up shop in Egypt, and by the kickbacks that, although not legal, have to be paid for things to work properly.

In the Egyptian economy, influence (called *wasta*) is what often gets things done. Wasta can mean simply having the right connections, like having personal or business ties that make it easy to win a contract, for example. It can mean paying the kickbacks or bribes that can grease the wheels if a businessman lacks personal connections. And wasta is part of Egypt's *bakshiish* economy. Bakshiish means tip, but it is often expected even if no service is provided, or to supplement the income of a person providing a service. For example, a visitor would pay admission to visit an ancient Egyptian monument and then would pay bakshiish—half a dollar or a dollar, perhaps—to the site's guard, who would show some of its attractions (whether the visitor wanted him to or not) and then whisper "bakshiish?"

Few foreigners traveling in Egypt ever get mad about paying out such trifling amounts to Egyptians, particularly when they appreciate how meager the locals' incomes are.

Membership in the Gezira Club, on Cairo's Gezira Island, is affordable only for Egypt's wealthiest people.

Most Americans would have a hard time imagining the salaries Egyptians get by on; typical middle-class salaries range between $100 and $400 per month (of course the costs of living are much lower than in the United States). Many people moonlight, or work second jobs, for example as taxi drivers. There are some very rich people in Egypt, too. One of the criticisms of Sadat's infitah policy, and of Egypt today, is that a select few have enriched themselves with lucrative business contracts, while the masses have lost ground or failed to make progress economically. The apparent disparities between the haves and have-nots in Egypt have grown. The visitor to Egypt sees flashy Mercedes cars and other showy signs of wealth, appearing quite out of place where city and village people struggle to make a living. While living space is notoriously cramped, costly, and difficult to find for the great majority of Egyptians, a select few have second and even third summer or winter homes in the countryside. There are fears that at some point popular resentment against the wealthy class could turn into riots or greater civil conflict in Egypt.

Egypt is of course an agricultural country—most of its people are rural—and one would expect farming to be among its leading economic assets. Egypt's fertile soils produce cereals (mainly wheat, maize, rice, and barley), cotton, sugar cane, vegetables (notably tomatoes, eggplant, cucumber, spinach, beans, okra, and onions), fruits (especially oranges, tangerines, lemons, apricots, grapes, bananas, and mangoes), and forage plants. Cotton, rice, and maize (corn) are the leading commercial export or cash crops. Egypt was once a considerable exporter of these and other agricultural products. Since the 1970s, however, Egypt has imported more food than it has exported, and the imbalance in favor of imports is growing steadily (food makes up more than 30 percent of Egypt's import expenditures). Most of the wheat, the country's staple cereal, for example, comes from the United States. The basic problem is the one that bedevils almost every effort Egypt makes to develop: The population is growing, and any gains that are made economically are quickly eaten up by that growth.

Egypt's approach to this dilemma has long been to try to increase the number of crops grown on its agricultural land and to expand its land area in cultivation. The biggest effort was the construction of the Aswan High Dam. It has been a mixed blessing for Egypt. On the plus side, it converted about a million acres of land in the Nile Valley and the Nile Delta from seasonal to perennial irrigation, meaning that two or three crops, instead of just one, could be grown each year. The area under cultivation has also increased by about a million acres,

Egyptian clover or *berseem* is the main crop grown as livestock fodder.

especially through the reclamation of desert land: With more water available, it became possible to irrigate the desert fringes of the Nile Valley and delta, particularly the area just west of the delta, between Cairo and Alexandria. Hydroelectricity for the country's commercial and residential needs is produced at the dam's power station (it generates about 25 percent of the country's electricity). The dam prevents destructive floods and provides water during periods of drought. On the negative side, farmers tend to overuse the always-available water, therefore accidentally adding too much salt to their fertile land—the salts are contained in the water and are left behind as the water evaporates. Farmers now have to buy expensive artificial fertilizers because the free fertilizer provided by the Ethiopian silt is now locked up behind the dam. Those silts gave nourishment to sardines in the Mediterranean Sea, off the shore of the Nile Delta, but the sardine fishing industry has come to end because the silts are gone. Mediterranean Sea water has begun to erode away land from the Nile Delta, because the silts are not rebuilding the delta's headland. Land reclamation has proven disappointing. Just getting water to the desert does not make its sands fertile. The inputs have been costly and the returns few: comprising about 13 percent of Egypt's total cultivated area, reclaimed lands contribute only 2 percent of the nation's total agricultural output. Many of Nubia's archaeological monuments were drowned by Lake Nasser, or, like Abu Simbel, had to be relocated to higher ground. Overall, however, Egyptians defend the decision to build the Aswan High Dam and argue that its benefits outweigh its problems.

Land reclamation west of the Nile Delta has been one of the multipronged efforts Egypt has undertaken to conquer and develop its deserts. Another is to increase cultivation and settlement in what Egyptians call the New Valley (*Wadi Gadeed*), the oases depressions of Kharga and Dakhla. They are judged to be underpopulated relative to the Nile Valley and delta, and so efforts are underway to draw settlers from the overcrowded Nile region by developing petroleum and mineral industries and increasing the cultivable area of these oases—mainly by drilling new wells, but also recently by bringing freshwater from Lake Nasser by canal in the so-called Tuskha Project. Another canal carries Nile water from the eastern delta into the northern Sinai Peninsula, where there are plans to resettle as many as a million inhabitants from the Nile region.

Still another effort focuses on the satellite cities, a series of new settlements constructed in desert areas, especially east and west of the Nile Delta. These were meant to relieve one of Egypt's great problems, the urban primacy of Cairo. The country's capital is a classic primate city, meaning Cairo has more people

With funding from the United States, the Ptolemaic temple of Philae, situated on an island between the low and high dams at Aswan, was cut up and moved to higher ground. Here the disassembled blocks were awaiting their final move.

than Egypt's second and third largest cities combined. Practically everything and everybody gravitates to Cairo, because that is where most of the country's jobs and services are located. The problem is that such urban primacy has a snowball effect: The opportunities attract more and more people, and the city keeps growing, so the government pours more and more resources into trying to keep up with the growing population. Cairo's impressive new subway system is part of that effort.

All of that attention to Cairo means that development

Cairo's efficient, French-designed subway system is helping to relieve some of the city's notorious traffic congestion. This is one of the underground stations.

elsewhere in the country is being neglected, and the increasing crowding and pollution in Cairo reduces the quality of life there. Meanwhile, Cairo's expansion is actually eating up quality farmland in a country that cannot afford to lose any. The satellite cities were meant to tackle these problems: New jobs and services would be created in them so that people would not have to move to Cairo; they would relieve the crowding in the Nile Valley and not consume farmland; and they would offer people cleaner air and greater quality of life than Cairo does. The problem has been that not enough people want to live in these new desert cities. Despite the lower costs of living and their other amenities in the desert, Egyptians prefer to live in the Nile area—especially in Cairo—where the action is. Egyptian distaste for the desert goes back to Pharaonic times, and it is a deep-seated cultural preference that has proven hard to change.

During Ramadan nights, people of Cairo throng to the square outside the
al-Hussein congregational mosque to listen to sermons, peruse religious literature,
and indulge in sweets. The festive tents come down after the holiday.

# 7

# Living in Egypt Today

L ife in Egypt today is a series of challenges that most Egyptians take on with characteristic good humor. That sense of humor combined with extraordinary patience help Egyptians cope with conditions that could make almost anybody break down in tears or cry out in anger. The overcrowding, the struggle to make a living, the burden of waiting for almost everything because too many people are trying to use limited services at the same time—these are features of everyday life that Egyptians shrug off with a smile. Their faith and their strong sense of family and friendship give them that fortitude.

To grow up in Egypt is to grow up blessed with family. Kinship ties are extremely important. In American society, it is common for brothers and sisters to live in different cities if not different states, and for children to leave home once they reach 18, seeing their parents less frequently. In Egypt, all the family members try to stay in the closest contact possible, and it is considered an emotional hardship when sons or daughters go to live and work in distant cities or countries. Parents lavish enormous affection on their children—what Americans call quality time is the norm in the Egyptian family. Then children look after their parents when their turn comes. There are no retirement homes, and elderly parents are taken in and cared for by the children until their lives end. Aunts, uncles, nephews, nieces, and cousins are also part of the daily scene in the Egyptian household.

Marriages are generally strong in Egypt; reflecting the value placed on family life, there is a low divorce rate. Gender roles are what Americans would call traditional. The man is expected to have the job, and the woman is expected to be the caretaker of the home and children. A lot of Egyptian women do work, particularly in the cities, but for many the job ends with marriage.

Finding a spouse in Egypt is a different process than it is in the United States. Parents have much say in what partner a son or daughter should have. Sometimes they negotiate an arranged marriage, finding a suitable bride or groom based on kinship. Traditionally, the ideal marriage has been between first cousins: A man should marry his father's brother's daughter, or his mother's brother's daughter. These unions are infrequent enough that genetic consequences are limited. The closeness of this ideal arrangement is, however, a good indicator of how close kinship bonds are in Egypt.

In the arranged marriage, which is more common in villages than in cities, love is expected to develop as time passes. As Egyptians see it, this is far better than falling madly in love at first sight, only to discover incompatibilities over time, and end a relationship in divorce. Where marriages are not arranged, there is dating, but it is quite different than typical courtship in the United States. For example, a son or daughter must get his or her parents' consent before going on a date. The dates are chaperoned—a brother or uncle or father accompanies the boy and girl to a film or restaurant, for example. Premarital sex is frowned upon, particularly because it can bring dishonor to a family. Honor is extremely important in Egyptian as in all Arab societies, and illicit relationships are among the most dishonorable acts.

Boy meets girl and parents approve is not the end of the courtship story. From the start, the groom is expected to be able to accommodate and care for his bride financially. This can be a huge challenge in Egypt's difficult economy. The man has to find a secure job and then save enough money to be able to make a down payment on an apartment. This can take years, and because of this men end up marrying much later than they would without these requirements. It is also customary, especially in the villages, for the groom to present his wife with a dowry, often called a bride-price. This could be cash, livestock, or other assets and represents some initial wealth that the wife may claim exclusively as her own.

Friendship, like family, is a strong institution in Egypt. Men and women develop intensely close bonds with others that can last a lifetime. Friends often call each other brothers or sisters. It is very rare for a man to have a close woman friend, or vice versa. Gender distance and separation are encouraged or enforced at every stage of life in Egypt—boys and girls are often educated separately, and public facilities are often segregated by sex. This separation is in keeping with the general Islamic sense of honor and propriety. Recent years have seen a growing embrace of fundamental Islamic values. For example, many more women wear the headscarf, or *hijab,* now than was true a decade or two ago.

Just being with family and friends is the favorite activity of most Egyptians. They are an extremely sociable and outgoing people and regard Americans as rather shy and retiring in comparison. Egyptians do not hesitate to open up a friendly conversation with anyone, and their "personal space" is closer than it is among Americans. Men greet men with hugs and kisses. Their handshakes linger, or they hold hands. Women do the same, and there is no awkwardness about that—these are expressions of friendship in Egypt.

Egypt is the music and film capital of the Arab world, and Egyptians are passionate about songs and movies. When the country's most beloved singer, Um Kalthum, died in 1975, there was an unprecedented national outpouring of grief. Her tapes are still best-sellers in Egypt. Egyptian film stars— including Omar Sharif, who also made it big in Western film roles—are the country's biggest celebrities. There are theaters all over the big cities, and video rentals are also strong. Televisions are in most urban Egyptian homes and are becoming more common in villages. Egyptians delight in soap operas, and recounting the actors' latest tribulations is a favorite topic of conversation. Educated Egyptians are avid readers, and Egypt boasts some of the Arab world's greatest writers. These include Naguib Mahfouz, a Nobel prizewinner whose translated works can be found in most bookstores in the United States.

Egyptians love sports, particularly soccer—which they call football. The rivalries between city soccer teams ignite passions among the fans, and the entire country rallies behind its national team during the annual World Cup playoffs. Egyptians are not great outdoors people— hiking and camping are not popular activities, for example—but they do enjoy day trips to Mediterranean or Red Sea beaches, or to the few green spaces in Cairo, especially the zoo.

As Egypt is a mainly Muslim country, the major holidays are Islamic: the 'Iyd al-Adha, or Feast of the Sacrifice, following the conclusion of the annual pilgrimage to Mecca; and the 'Iyd al-Fitr, or Feast of the Breaking of the Fast, following the end of the fast during the month of Ramadan. The prophet Muhammad's birthday (Mulid an-Nabi) is another important

The Egyptian government is committed to improving the literacy rate in the nation. More people are literate now than before the 1952 revolution. About 66 percent of Egypt's men and 40 percent of its women are literate.

Muslim feast day. There are also pre-Islamic holidays, including the springtime festival called Sniffing the Breeze (*Sham an-Nasiiim*). During each of these holidays, large embroidered tents are erected on city streets, within which sweets, toys, and holiday decorations are sold.

Almost every Egyptian has a sweet tooth. Even a cup of tea is prepared with a few heaps of sugar. The country's most widely consumed foods are boiled fava beans (*fuul*) and deep-fried chick peas (*taamiya*). Western fast-food restaurants, including McDonald's and KFC, are common in the bigger cities, but the traditional Egyptian fast-foods are fuul, taamiya, and *kushri,* a spicy macaroni and lentil dish. Meats are too expensive for most people to consume frequently, but popular meat dishes are made from lamb or mutton and include *shawerma,* grilled lamb served with tomatoes on a hot bun.

Islamic traditions frown upon intoxicants, and alcoholism and drug use are rare in Egypt. Beer, wine, and spirits are offered only in tourist restaurants, and they are sold in a few government stores, or discreetly in some urban supermarkets. As both intravenous drug use and homosexuality are uncommon in Egypt, the rate of HIV/AIDS infection is low.

Egyptians do have some health problems, however. Smoking is almost universal among men. There are very few public restrictions or warnings about smoking, and although statistics are not available, cancer death rates are believed to be high. Egyptians enjoy a medium quality of life when compared with the other countries of the world. The average life expectancy is 66, compared with 77 in the United States, and 45 in Afghanistan. The United Nations' Human Development Index rates Egypt's overall quality of life as 119th out of the world's 174 countries (with Canada as number 1, and Sierra Leone as number 174). This index goes beyond simple per capita gross national product or income standards to evaluate aspects of the human experience. It includes gender-related development and gender empowerment, human poverty, trends in human development and economic growth, progress in survival, health profile, education profile, access to information flows, economic performance, resource flows, resource use, aid and debt receipt, demographic trends, energy use, environmental profile, food security and nutrition, job security, political life, crime, personal distress, gender and education, gender and work, and women's political participation. Neither at the top nor at the bottom when measured by these standards, Egyptians know they could be better off, but make do—often very creatively and with a great sense of humor—with what they have. Visitors see immediately that Egyptians laugh a lot and enjoy exchanging jokes, even in the most trying circumstances—stuck in a traffic jam in Cairo, for instance, which is likely to be a visitor's first experience in the country.

That long ride offers a microcosm of life in Egypt today. The driver is a middle-aged man with a university degree in engineering. He works at the Ministry of Agriculture in a desk job that pays him $75 a month, not nearly enough to keep up with rent, food, and clothing for his wife and five children. With the driving he can earn a total of $200 a month. But he is not complaining so much as he is asking his passenger about where he is from and about his family. At the start of the ride, the driver may have said that the fare would be E£5, but by the end of the ride, the visitor may have to politely decline the driver's invitation to dine with him and his family, and the driver has refused to accept any payment.

Poor rural migrants to Cairo often have difficulty finding a place to live, and may spent time as squatters in makeshift street camps.

# Egypt Looks Ahead

**M**oving forward, the people of this "antique land" are confronted with many local, regional, and global challenges to their well being. There are pressing social, economic, and political issues for the country's leaders and citizens to deal with. This chapter provides a brief discussion of some of the steps that the majority of Egypt's observers insist the country should take forward.

The most difficult problems are economic. Prospects for Egypt's poor, who make up half the population, have not improved in recent years. The middle class, too, has made little progress. Most of the economic benefits have gone to the wealthiest 10 percent of the population. Unless this widening gap begins to narrow, chances for political unrest and violence will increase. Observers agree that Egypt's government must do more to improve the lives of Egypt's underprivileged. More government jobs and services need to be created in the poorest parts of the country, particularly the villages and towns of Upper (southern) Egypt. The government will have to preserve and even expand its social security net for the poor by subsidizing their basic food and clothing needs, rather than continue to look for ways to cut the subsidies. Presumably, reducing expenditures on defense could free up more money for this purpose. And, because much of Egypt's rural poverty is a result of too few agricultural resources, improvements in farming must be made. The continued expansion of cities and towns into Egypt's precious limited farmland must be stopped. The current emphasis on large-scale efforts to reclaim desert land should be reevaluated, because of the enormous cost and typically low returns of these projects. Worldwide experience suggests that more benefits may come from small-scale, local efforts to improve existing farming technology.

Perhaps the most serious threat to Egypt's economic well being is population growth. Even though it has slowed markedly in recent decades, the population growth rate is still high, and Egypt's population is expected to grow by two-thirds in the next half century. This expected surge in people means that the country faces a huge struggle just to break even, much less gain ground economically. Again, more attention to the root problem of poverty is essential to reduce birth rates. Women, in particular rural women, need more education—there is a worldwide correlation between greater female literacy and lower birth rates. This will require some fundamental cultural changes. Parents will need to be convinced that their daughters can and should go to school—now they tend to hold the girls back with the belief that "their place is in the home" and therefore they need not attend class.

Egypt's campaign to lower birth rates emphasizes that fewer children mean more amenities. This sign in Cairo's main square reads, "The Choice Is Yours: Family Planning, For the Sake of a Better Life."

Egypt's past and potential domestic unrest also has roots in the country's poverty. Islamist extremism originated in Upper Egypt, the poorest part of the country, and made progress as extremists argued that Islamic law was the one true alternative to a political system that benefited mainly the wealthy. To defuse future Islamist revolt, the Egyptian government will have to do more than arrest and imprison

Islamists, which is the main method used now. More genuine attention to the plight of the poor, and more concessions to the demands of moderate Islamists to participate in Egypt's political life, will be needed. All across the political spectrum there are pleas for greater freedom of expression and opportunities for political power. Egypt risks losing its place as the capital of Arab culture unless its intellectuals and artists are permitted to express themselves without fear of imprisonment. Political repression can also pose threats to the stability of the government, as Islamists or others turn to violence as their only means of expression.

Egypt's central place in the regional and international strategic arena seems secure for the near future, but there are long-term dangers. The United States does not want this demographic giant of 70-plus million to become unfriendly to its interests and is likely to continue sending large amounts of economic aid to Egypt. The United States relies on Egypt in particular to mediate in the Israeli-Palestinian dispute, and as long as the conflict goes unresolved the U.S.-Egypt economic partnership should be strong (ironically, then, regional peace could be bad economically for Egypt). At the same time, Egypt does not want to be seen by its Arab neighbors as a puppet of the United States. Its struggle to maintain some political independence from the United States may be seen in particular in Egypt's view of Iraq. The United States wants Egypt to support economic sanctions and be ready to apply military pressure against the regime of Saddam Hussein, but the Mubarak government answers that U.S. policy only hurts ordinary Iraqis. Egypt was also slow to embrace any U.S. expansion outside Afghanistan of the war on terrorism following the September 2001 attacks in which, as the opening of this book pointed out, some Egyptians were involved.

"There were very many things in Egypt which filled me

with astonishment," the Greek geographer and historian Herodotus wrote in the fifth century B.C.E. Egypt is still and promises always to be a land of wonders and of the good natured and giving people called Egyptian.

# Facts at a Glance

| | |
|---|---|
| **Location** | Northeastern corner Africa and southwest Asia (Sinai Peninsula) |
| **Geographic coordinates general** | 27 degrees north, 30 degrees east |
| **Land Area** | 386,662 square miles (1,001,450 square kilometers) |
| **Coastlines** | 1,613 miles (2,689 kilometers), on Mediterranean Sea, Gulf of Suez, Gulf of Aqaba, and Red Sea |
| **Climate** | desert; hot, dry summers with mild winters, rainy in north |
| **Terrain** | mountainous igneous rocks in Sinai and Eastern Desert; sedimentary plateaus in Western Desert; Nile Valley runs north south through limestone plateau |
| **Elevation extremes** | lowest point, Qattara Depression, 173 feet (133 meters) below sea level; highest point, Jebel Katarina, 8,715 feet, (2,641 meters) |
| **Natural resources** | petroleum, natural gas, iron ore, phosphates, manganese, limestone, gypsum, talc, asbestos, lead, zinc |
| **Arable land** | 2 percent |
| **Irrigated land** | 12,984 square miles (32,460 square kilometers) (1993) |
| **Population** | 69.8 million (2001) |
| **Birth rate** | 28 per thousand (2001) |
| **Death rate** | 7 per thousand (2001) |
| **Annual population change rate** | 2.1 percent (2001) |
| **Projected rate of population change** | 64 percent (2001-2050) |
| **Infant mortality** | 44 deaths per 1000 live births |
| **Population under age 15** | 36 percent |
| **Life expectancy** | 66 (average for males and females) |
| **Urban population** | 43 percent |
| **Gross national income purchasing power parity per capita** | $3,460 (1999) |
| **Gross domestic income real growth rate** | 5 percent (1999) |
| **Gross domestic product by sector** | Agriculture, 17 percent; Industry, 32 percent; Services, 51 percent (1999) |
| **Unemployment** | 11.5 percent (1999) |
| **Industries** | Textiles, food processing, tourism, chemicals, hydrocarbons, construction, cement, metals |
| **Export commodities** | Crude oil and petroleum products, cotton, textiles, metal products, chemicals |

| | |
|---|---|
| **Export partners** | European Union 35 percent, Middle East 17 percent, Afro-Asian countries 14 percent; United States 12 percent (1999) |
| **Import commodities** | Machinery and equipment, foodstuffs, chemicals, wood products, fuels |
| **Import partners** | European Union 36 percent; United States 14 percent; Afro-Asian countries 14 percent, Middle East 6 percent (1999) |
| **External debt** | $31 billion (2000) |
| **Currency** | Egyptian pound; exchange rate 3.84 pounds per U.S. dollar (2001) |
| **Television broadcast stations** | 98 (1995) |
| **Televisions** | 7.7 million (1997) |
| **Railways** | 2,973 miles (4,955 kilometers) |
| **Highways** | 25,600 miles (64,000 kilometers) |
| **Airports** | 90 (2000) |
| **Military manpower available** | Males age 15-49, 18,562,994 (2001) |
| **Military expenditure percent of gross domestic product** | 4.1 percent (2000) |
| **Ethnic groups** | Eastern Hamitic stock (Egyptian, Bedouin, and Berber), 99 percent; Greek, Nubian, Armenian, other European, 1 percent |
| **Religions** | Muslim (mostly Sunni), 94 percent; Coptic Christian and other, 6 percent |
| **Male literacy** | (over age 15 can read and write): 63.6 percent (1995) |
| **Female literacy** | (over age 15 can read and write): 38.8 percent (1995) |
| **Government** | Republic |
| **Capital city** | Cairo |
| **Independence** | 28 February 1922 (from the United Kingdom) |
| **Legal system** | based on English common law, Islamic law, and Napoleonic codes |
| **Suffrage** | 18 years of age; universal |
| **Executive branch** | Chief of State (President Hosni Mubarak, since October 1981); Head of Government, Prime Minister Atef Obeid (since October 1999) |
| **Legislative branch** | Bicameral system consists of People's Assembly, or Majlis al-Sha'ab, and the Advisory Council, or Majlis al-Shura |
| **Judicial branch** | Supreme Constitutional Court |
| **Political parties** | National Democratic Party (President Hosni Mubarak, leader); Nasserist Arab Democratic Party; National Progressive Unionist Grouping; Socialist Liberal Party; formation of political parties must be approved by government |

# History at a Glance

| | |
|---|---|
| **3100 B.C.E.** | Upper and Lower Egypt united under King Menes. |
| **2700–2200** | Old Kingdom—during this time the Egyptians built the Great Pyramid and Sphinx. |
| **1570–1090** | New Kingdom—The pharaoh Ramses II builds enormous monuments to himself throughout Egypt. |
| **332–30** | Ptolemaic (Greek) Period—Alexander the Great rules Egypt. |
| **30 B.C.E. to 324 A.D.** | Egypt was ruled by the Romans. |
| **641** | Arabs conquer Egypt and introduce the Islamic religion. |
| **969–1171** | The Fatimid Dynasty rules Egypt and moves the capital from Alexandria to Cairo. |
| **1171–1250** | Saladin defeated the Fatimids and established the Ayyubid Dynasty. |
| **1250–1382** | Bahri Mameluke seize control. |
| **1516–1798** | Ottoman Turks rule. |
| **1798** | Napoleon Bonaparte enters Egypt. |
| **1805–1848** | Reign of Muhammad Ali. |
| **1848–1922** | Reigns of Ibrahim Abbas I, Said, Ismail, Khedive Tawfiq, Khedive Abbas II, Ahmed Fu'ad. |
| **1882** | British colonization of Egypt begins. |
| **1922** | Independence from the United Kingdom; accession of King Fu'ad I. |
| **1948** | War with Israel. |
| **1952** | Gamal Abdel Nasser leads a revolution that ousts King Farouk. |
| **1956–70** | Presidency of Nasser; 1956 Suez Crisis and war with Britain, France, and Israel; 1967 war with Israel. |
| **1971–81** | Presidency of Anwar Sadat; 1973 war with Israel; 1979 Camp David peace treaty with Israel; the Sinai Peninsula is returned to Egypt. |
| **1981–Present** | Presidency of Hosni Mubarak |

**Allah:** Arabic for God

**bakshiish:** tip

**caliph:** successor to the Prophet Muhammad

**corvée:** system of forced labor

**fellaah (singular), fellaahiin (plural):** peasant farmer(s)

**fuul:** fava beans

**khamsiin:** "50 days" of hot, sand bearing winds, March to May

**hijab:** headscarf for women

**hajj:** pilgrimage to Mecca

**infitah:** Egypt's "opening" to international markets, beginning in the 1970s

**'Iyd al-Adha:** feast of the Sacrifice following pilgrimage to Mecca

**'Iyd al-Fitr:** feast of the Breaking of the Fast following the month of Ramadan.

**kushri:** macaroni and lentils

**Masr:** Arabic for Egypt and Cairo

**mastaba:** bench-shaped tomb of nobleman during the Old Kingdom

**medina:** classic walled city of the Muslim Middle East

**Mulid an-Nabi:** prophet Muhammad's birthday

**shaduf:** weighted lever and bucket, used for lifting water from canal to field

**Sham an-Nasiiim:** springtime "Sniffing the Breeze" feast

**shawerma:** grilled lamb

**suq:** marketplace

**taamiya:** deep-fried chick peas

**wasta:** personal connections or other influence that get business done

**zabaaliin:** Cairo's Coptic Christian trash collectors

# Further Reading

Anderson, Ewan W. *The Middle East: Geography and Geopolitics.* London: Routledge, 2000.

Beaumont, Peter, Gerald H. Blake and Wagstaff ,Malcolm J. *The Middle East: A Geographical Study* (Second Edition). New York: Halsted, 1988.

Bill, James A. and Springbord, Robert. *Politics in the Middle East* (Third Edition). Glenview, I.L.: Scott, Foresman/Little, Brown, 1990.

Bowen, Donna Lee and Early, Evelyn A. *Everyday Life in the Muslim Middle East.* Bloomington: Indiana University Press, 1993.

Breasted, James Henry. *A History of Egypt.* New York: Bantam, 1964.

Goldschmidt, Arthur. *A Concise History of the Middle East.* Boulder, C.O.: Westview Press, 1991

Goodman, Steven M. and Peter L. Meininger eds. *The Birds of Egypt.* Oxford: Oxford University Press, 1989.

Held, Colbert C. *Middle East Patterns: Places, People and Politics* (Third Edition). Boulder, C.O.: Westview Press, 2000.

Lippman, Thomas W. *Egypt After Nasser.* New York: Paragon House, 1989.

Rawlinson, George, translator. *Herodotus Histories.* Ware, Hertfordshire: Wordsworth, 1996.

Waterbury, John. *Hydropolitics of the Nile Valley.* Syracuse, N.Y.: Syracuse University Press, 1979.

Youssef, Hisham and Rodenbeck, John, eds. *Insight Guides: Egypt.* Boston, M.A.: Houghton Mifflin, 1997.

# Index

## About the Author

**JOSEPH HOBBS** is a Professor of Geography at the University of Missouri-Columbia. He has spent many years in Egypt, studying Egyptology and Arabic and doing field research on the natural environments and cultures of the Bedouin peoples of the Eastern Desert and the Sinai Peninsula. His major books on Egypt are *Bedouin Life in the Egyptian Wilderness* and *Mount Sinai* (both University of Texas Press).

**CHARLES F. "FRITZ" GRITZNER** is Distinguished Professor of Geography at South Dakota State University. He is now in his fifth decade of college teaching and research. Much of his career work has focused on geographic education. Fritz has served as both president and executive director of the National Council for Geographic Education and has received the Council's George J. Miller Award for Distinguished Service.